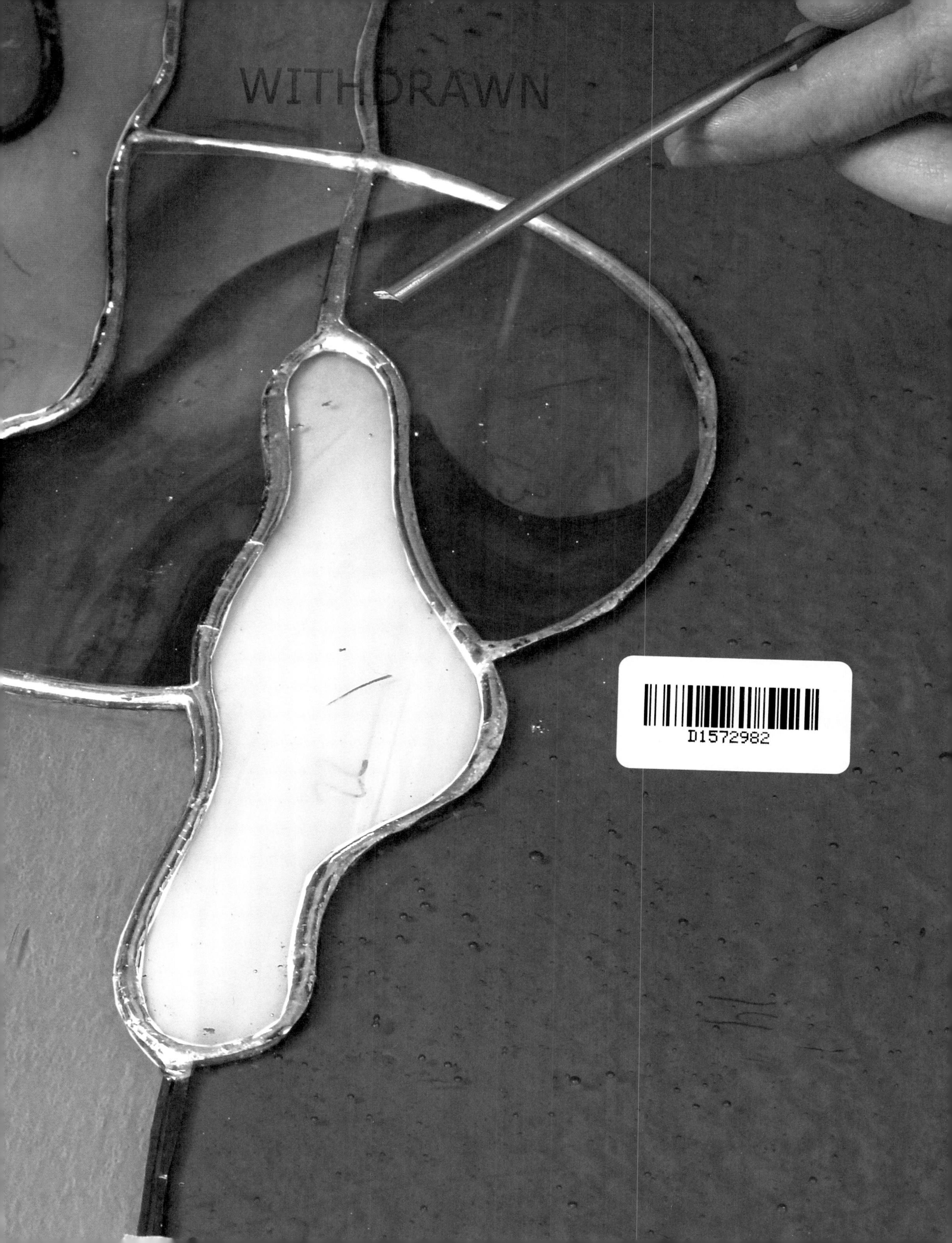

leaded

glass

Projects and techniques

JULIA RODRIGUEZ

EVA PASCUAL

4880 Lower Valley Road • Atglen, PA 19310

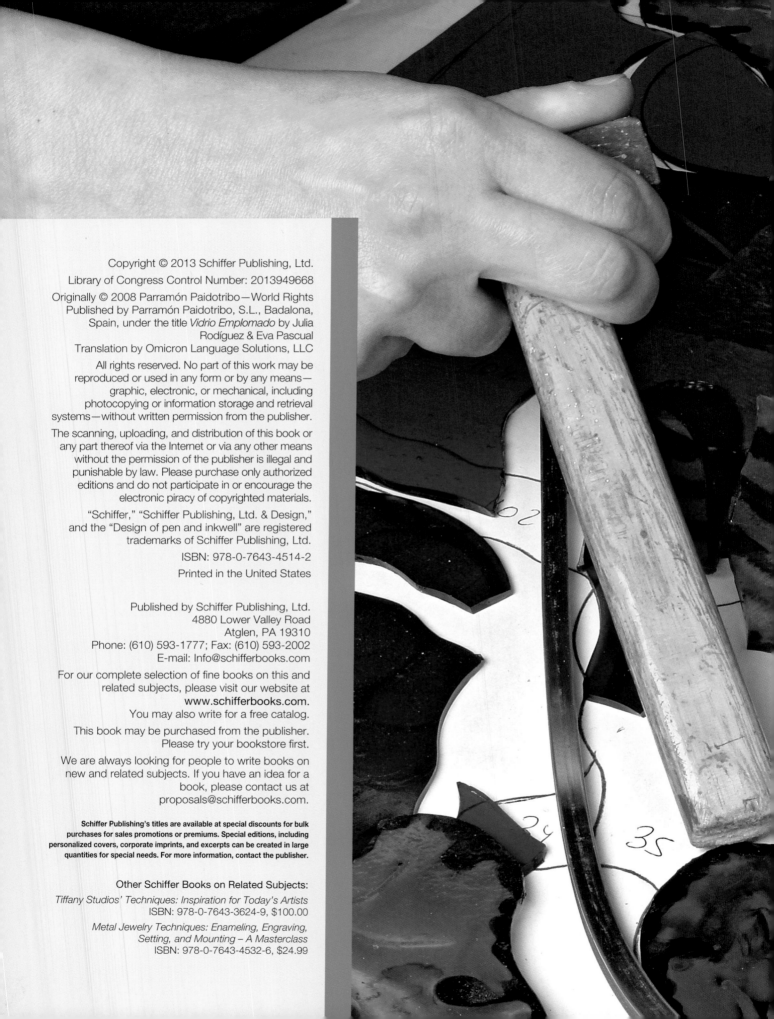

Library of Congress Control Number: 2013949668

Originally © 2008 Parramón Paidotribo—World Rights
Published by Parramón Paidotribo, S.L., Badalona,
Spain, under the title *Vidrio Emplomado* by Julia
Rodríguez & Eva Pascual

Translation by Omicron Language Solutions, LLC

ISBN: 978-0-7643-4514-2

Printed in the United States

Published by Schiffer Publishing, Ltd.
4880 Lower Valley Road
Atglen, PA 19310
Phone: (610) 593-1777; Fax: (610) 593-2002
E-mail: Info@schifferbooks.com

For our complete selection of fine books on this and
related subjects, please visit our website at
www.schifferbooks.com.
You may also write for a free catalog.

This book may be purchased from the publisher.
Please try your bookstore first.

We are always looking for people to write books on
new and related subjects. If you have an idea for a
book, please contact us at
proposals@schifferbooks.com.

Schiffer Publishing's titles are available at special discounts for bulk
purchases for sales promotions or premiums. Special editions, including
personalized covers, corporate imprints, and excerpts can be created in large
quantities for special needs. For more information, contact the publisher.

Other Schiffer Books on Related Subjects:

Tiffany Studios' Techniques: Inspiration for Today's Artists
ISBN: 978-0-7643-3624-9, $100.00

*Metal Jewelry Techniques: Enameling, Engraving,
Setting, and Mounting – A Masterclass*
ISBN: 978-0-7643-4532-6, $24.99

leaded
glass

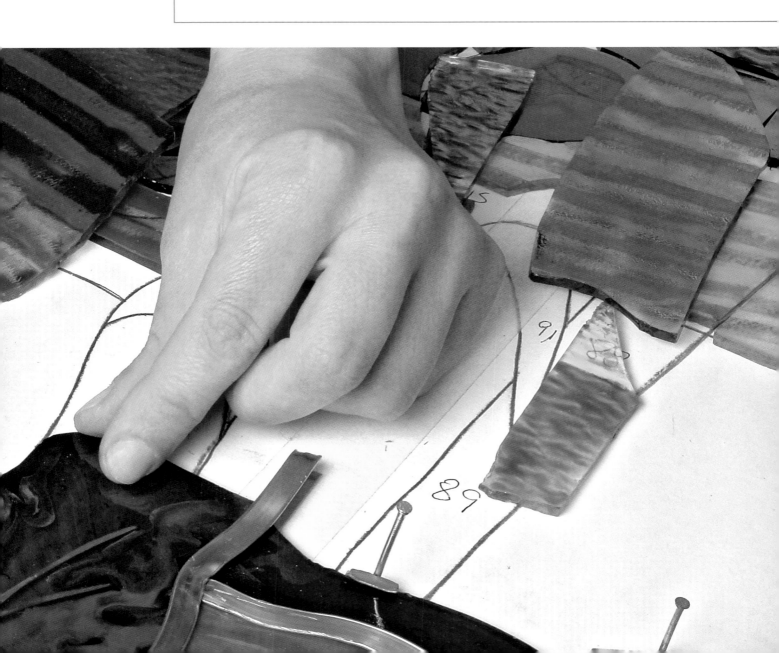

Materials
and tools

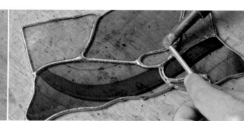

Basic techniques

Step by step

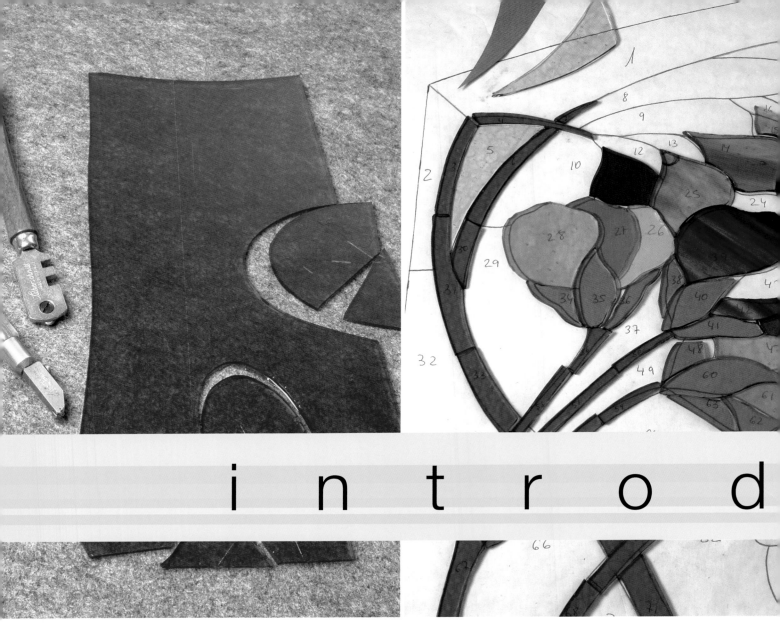

introd

This book brings together the main elements of the art of leaded glass. It explains in detail the underlying principles of this specialized field, providing an overall and detailed view of the methods and techniques from an educational viewpoint. This discipline, based on the creation of surfaces and objects by joining glass with a metal support, encompasses two different methods: lead and copper foil (also known as Tiffany). The creation of objects in leaded glass with either of these processes involves, in the majority of cases, preparatory work on the glass, applying different techniques in order to vary some of its characteristics or to give it some new ones. This book, focusing on the production of objects, is divided into four chapters.

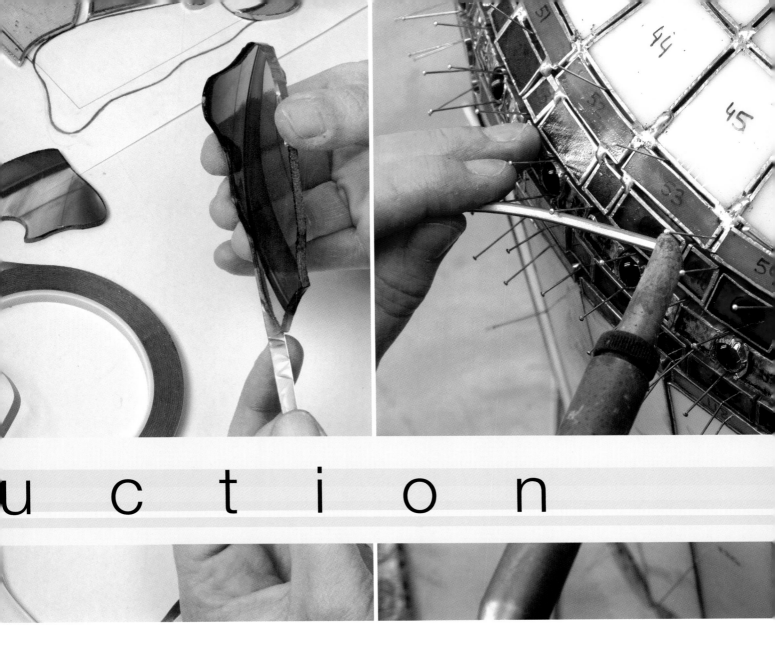

uction

The first shows the materials and tools grouped together according to their use, paying special attention to the main types of glass. Next, there is a chapter dedicated to basic techniques which deals with the design of the object and creation of models, as well as cutting and polishing and the different methods for working directly with glass. Naturally, the processes of the techniques for leading and copper foil are explained thoroughly, set out as a guide to facilitate the undertaking of any work. The third chapter brings together six examples of objects with step by step explanations to show the development of the complete process of each object. Lastly, there is an interesting gallery and a glossary which explains the main concepts used; additionally, a section of bibliographical resources that will be very useful for those who wish to deepen their knowledge of the topic by means of other sources.

In this chapter, the characteristics of the materials and tools used for creating stained glass objects are shown and explained in detail. First, the main types of glass are defined, offering a wide range of reference. Next, materials and tools for working directly with glass are presented and organized into groups according to their use: materials for support and joint work; glass treatments like enamels and patinas; tools for cutting and shaping glass; specific machines for glasswork; important safety measures; and finishing tools.

Materials and tools

Colored antique glass.

MATERIALS

Glass

This is a synthesized material composed of different raw materials: vitreous substance (silica, basic component of glass), flux (materials which facilitate the formation of the material and its fusion), stabilizers (to add hardness) and secondary materials (coloring or bleaching agents). It is obtained by supercooling the molten vitreous mass (formed by the different components), which is homogenous, amorphous and malleable, by blowing it or manipulating it through different procedures. Despite its solid appearance, glass is, chemically speaking, a supercooled liquid;its amorphous molecular structure makes it more similar to liquids than crystals. This peculiarity as a material defines its properties (for example, it is a hard solid but extremely fragile) and characteristics as regards its transparency and brilliance. There is a great variety of types of glass, depending on its appearance and the manufacturing processes used. Its type varies according to the individual maker. The next section looks at the main variations used in leaded glass work.

ANTIQUE GLASS

This name is given to glass which is blown, either by mouth or by industrial processes. It is made from the creation by heat of a cylinder (muff) which is opened and flattened to create a sheet of glass. Antique glass has special characteristics: a very shiny surface, rather uneven but smooth, with irregular thickness, bubbles and grooves. Each sheet is unique and has its own qualities, making it well suited to leaded glass work. When working on it the rounded edges are removed, as they can

Antique glass.

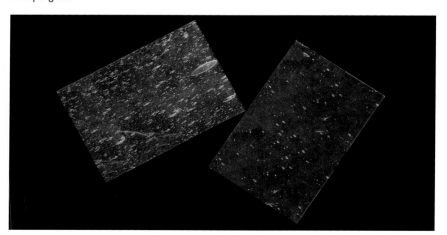

Cast glass.

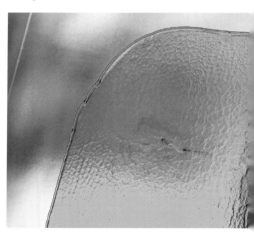

10

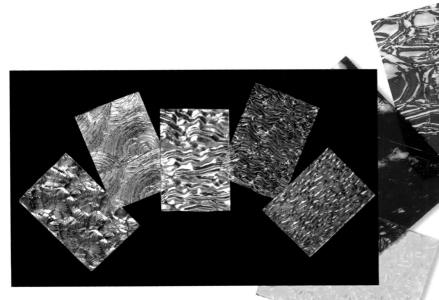

Textured glass with different textures.

Colored textured glass.

lead to stress and cause the glass to break.

CAST GLASS

Cast glass is the result of pouring the vitreous mass into a mold or onto a metal table and stretching it with a roller to turn it into a sheet.

TEXTURED GLASS

Textured glass is a variety of cast glass. If the roller has a raised textured surface, this will be transferred to one of the sides of the sheet of the mass, resulting in a sheet of glass which has one side which is textured and the other, resting in the mold, remains smooth. There is a great variety in the textures of this kind of glass: transparent, translucent, colorless, colored, etc.

MANUFACTURED GLASS

This is made by various different types of manufacturing processes such as stretching or floating. This consists of melting the components of the glass in a tank furnace and then passing it into a chamber with a bath of molten solder onto which the glass floats. It is stretched and moves on to be finished in the reheating furnace. Manufactured glass is perfectly smooth and uniform and the sheet has an even thickness throughout.

Colored transparent manufactured glass.

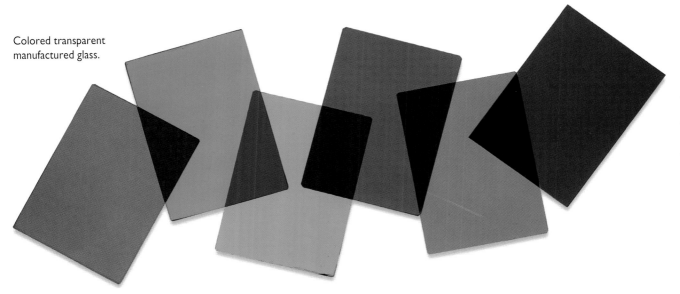

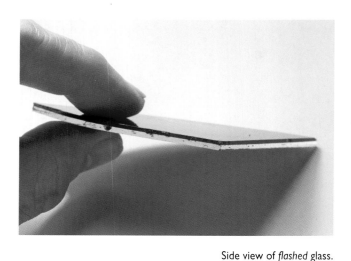

Side view of *flashed* glass.

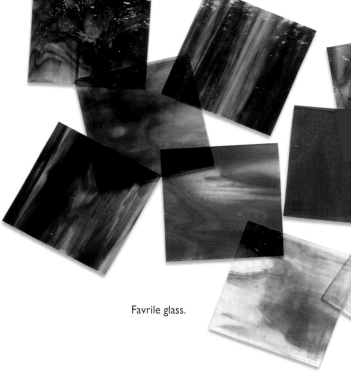

Favrile glass.

FLASHED GLASS

Flashed glass, also called folded glass, is formed of two layers, one of which is usually colorless, although there are also varieties with two color layers. It is well suited for creating chromatic effects and for, by means of various grinding techniques, obtaining different shades and tones of color.

OPALESCENT GLASS

Opalescent glass, also called opaline, is translucent or completely opaque, with a characteristic shine, similar to that of wax, and iridescent highlights. This milky colored glass is faintly reminiscent of alabaster, a type of marble, even though opaline refers to the opal, a highly valued translucent semi-precious stone which has a waxy, at times iridescent, shine. It can be of one or a number of colors, showing veins of a color different to that of the background. There are also semi-opalescent varieties which are more translucent than the opaline types.

FAVRILE GLASS

This type of glass is made during casting. It has a very particular appearance, with splashes of color, generally, mixed with white, usually opaline, or colorless glass. It produces interesting color and depth effects, depending on the direction of the cut and the layout and assembly of the work.

Semi-opalescent antique glass.

Opalescent glass of a single color.

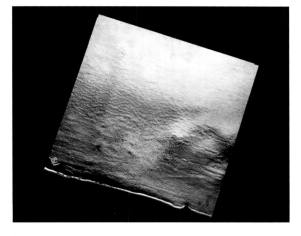

Iridescent glass.

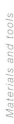

IRIDESCENT GLASS

Iridescent glass shows very particular coloration. The surface gives off an iridescent effect, creating rainbow hued reflections and brilliances. The optical effect consists in the light splitting in the seven primary colors, due to the phenomenon of interference or diffraction of the light. The glass reflects the light showing subtle contrasts of tones and different brilliances, resulting in a very interesting appearance in artistic terms.

MOLDED GLASS

This is the term given to pieces of glass of different types, reliefs and shapes, generally, achieved by putting the vitreous mass inside a mold to obtain the desired shape, although some can be made by turning or working on them by hand. The possibilities are endless, with discs being the most common. These are turned circular pieces with a blunt outside edge.

Discs.

Two-colored opalescent glass.

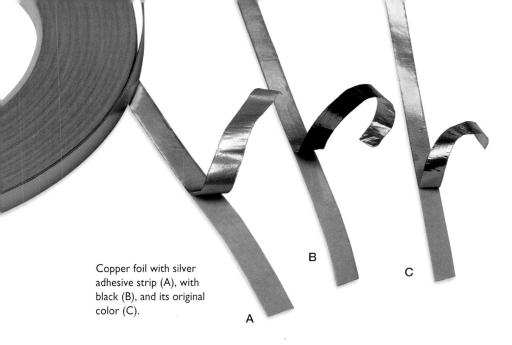

Copper foil with silver adhesive strip (A), with black (B), and its original color (C).

Different side views of lead came.

Materials for support and joints

Copper foil: this is used for the copper foil or Tiffany technique. It consists of a thin sheet of copper with adhesive on one side which allows it to be fixed onto and cover the edges of pieces of glass. It is produced in rolls of different widths for glass of different thickness and also with different colors on the adhesive part such as copper, black or silver which are used for transparent or mirror glass.

Lead came: strips or rods of lead are made up of a central core and sections called wings or lips. The core is a vertical shape which gives resistance and rigidity to the strip; its surfaces are grooved or indented, so as to hold the glass and putty more effectively. It is the lips or wings, once rounded, which hold the glass. The gap which they fit into is called the channel or heart. Lead comes in different shapes and with different sized wings.

Solder: this is a shiny white metal, very malleable and ductile, which melts easily. It is used to solder the joints of the leaded and copper foil pieces and comes in sticks. To solder the leaded pieces an alloy is used consisting of 50% solder and 50% lead; to join copper foil pieces alloy sticks of 60% solder and 40% lead are used.

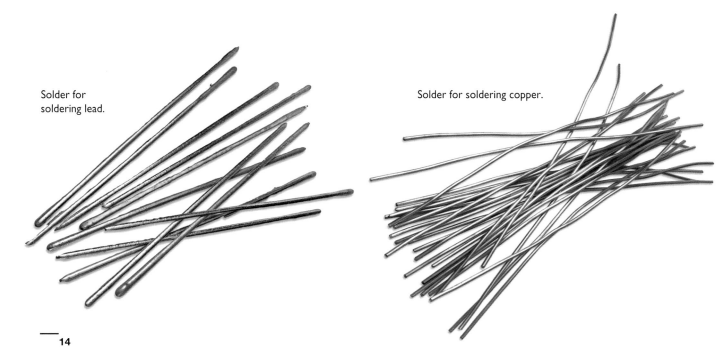

Solder for soldering lead.

Solder for soldering copper.

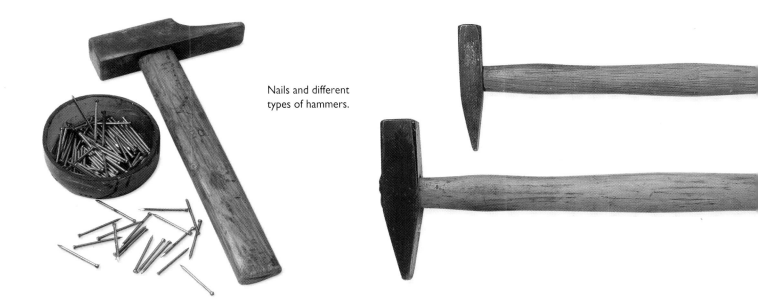

Nails and different types of hammers.

Hammer: this is used in leading to insert into the surface of the piece the ends of the nails or the tacks used to fix and hold the lead cames in place. They are also used as tools to help bang the edges of the glass with the end of the handle, fitting it completely into the lead, between the wings. There is a great variety of hammers, although the lighter ones are recommended, preferably with an iron head which is not very wide and with a wooden handle.

Lead knife: these are used to open up the lead came by inserting them inside the wings, as if to straighten it, pressing against the heart. These are also called openers, tools made of metal or durable stiff plastic with pointed ends. There are different types of lead knives; plastic ones can be flat and rectangular with points at both ends like a knife, so-called double-ended, or with one end in the shape of a palette knife and the other with a slightly curved outer edge. This type is often called a "bird",

due to the shape of a beak and a tail. Both lead knives can be used as knives to press and spread the copper foil already laid on the edges and side of the glass.

Wire brush: this is a brush with wire bristles which is very useful for cleaning old lead before applying new solder and for cleaning already prepared pieces. These brushes can have iron or wire bristles, here an ordinary shoe cleaning brush.

B

A

Double ended lead knife (A) and pointed or "bird" knife (B).

Wire brush.

File.

Soldering iron for copper foil.

For **soldering**

Soldering irons: these are electric tools with a wooden or plastic handle into which a tube with a flat or bevelled copper head is inserted.
They are used for joining, with lead solder, the network of lead cames which hold the glass or the copper foil covering them. There are different types of soldering irons, some are specifically for lead and others for joining the copper foil. The soldering irons for lead are between 100 to 180 W (watts) and come with a tip into which a bar of copper is inserted. Some models work at 75 W; these are adequate for joining narrow pieces of lead and reach lower temperatures than other models, allowing the soldering to be easily controlled. There are also soldering irons with one head and others with two heads, called thermal soldering irons. These have a head with two branches, one has a rounded point for soldering sides, and the other is bevelled for soldering angles. They have a thermostat which regulates the temperature of the work to a maximum of 300°C.
Other soldering irons have a long bevelled point, and are used for small scale soldering work and joints in difficult nooks and crannies. The soldering irons for copper are tools using 75 or 80 W with a metal point, in some models it is iron, in a bevelled shape.
File: a tool with a textured steel blade and a plastic or metal handle. The blade is flat and rectangular with grooved surfaces. It is used for cleaning the outside of the copper bar of the soldering irons.

A

B

C

D

E

Lead soldering irons: flat headed (A), bevelled (B), flat headed soldering iron of 75 W (C), thermal soldering iron (D) pick soldering iron (E).

28

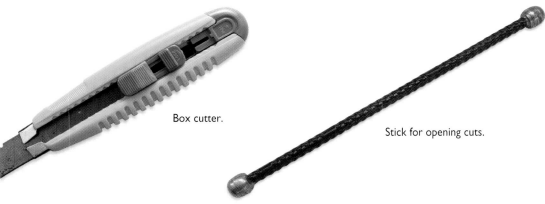

Box cutter.

Stick for opening cuts.

Supplementary **tools**

Stained glass pattern shears: this tool, also called template shears, are used in the preparatory processes of planning and designing, for making templates. They are special shears with three blades which make a double cut. They are made of steel and composed of two parts or blades; the double blade has a gap into which the single blade fits when it is closed. There are specialist shears for templates for lead work and others for copper foil work. The first have one blade of the same thickness of the heart of the lead came, so that

the same thickness is replicated in the templates, and these produce a cut of 1.75mm in width. The shears for copper work produce a 1 mm gap on the templates. These shears come in varieties specifically for lead or for copper or can be mixed, which are suitable for cutting both types of templates. The mixed type always have an interchangeable single blade.

Cutter: this is a knife with disposable blades with a plastic handle which houses a blade. It is used for making precise cuts, for cutting paper and card for plans and designs to scale.

Stick for opening up cuts: this is a special instrument, made in the studio. It consists of a rod of steel covered with a sheet of plastic with blobs of bronze soldered onto each end. It is used as an tool which is light and easy to control and with which cuts can be opened by tapping.

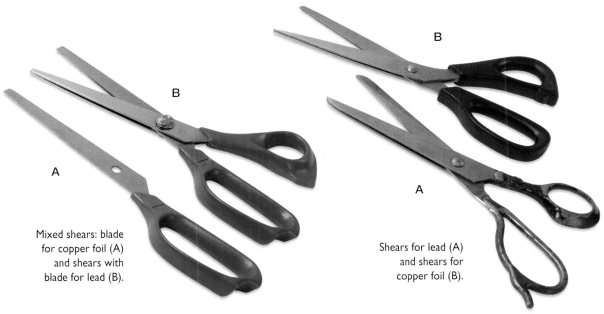

Mixed shears: blade for copper foil (A) and shears with blade for lead (B).

Shears for lead (A) and shears for copper foil (B).

Materials and tools

In this chapter, the basic techniques for creating works of glass with leading and copper tape are explained in detail. For each piece, the original design is shown, followed by the methods used to develop the project and bring it to life. By articulating these fundamentals of glasswork, this chapter will serve as a general guide for the development of your own projects.

básic

Techniques

PLAN AND DESIGN

The creation of works in leaded and copper foil glass require prior planning and an analysis of the idea by the artist, that is, a plan needs to be made that afterwards will be expressed in a detailed manner in the design. In the planning phase, a sketch or preparatory drawing is made which reflects in a more or less detailed way the idea of the work which will be undertaken. Then, using the sketch as a guide, the design is created.

Design and creation of models

Design

The sketch, in some cases, can be a drawing which gives expression to the object and does not differ that much from the subsequent design. However, sometimes, the design can serve to deepen the initial concept, allowing it to evolve, converting it into an aid to explore visual solutions, colors, textures and shapes. It is useful for thinking about and visualizing the piece and is essential for the creative process. The design, then, is the definitive plan, where the characteristics of the piece are expressed to scale and also the colors and the qualities of the glass, as well as the lines of leading or copper foil, the finish and the location of the work if it is not free standing. It is used for creating, by enlarging, the drawing to life size. In this sense, it is worth pointing out the facilities which technology offers, for example computer assisted design and machine copied designs.

Designs for lampshades. Originals by Julia Rodríguez. Ink and gouache on paper, 2002.

The designs reflect the colors of the glass and the lines of the lead. Design for a folding screen, by Julia Rodríguez, 2004.

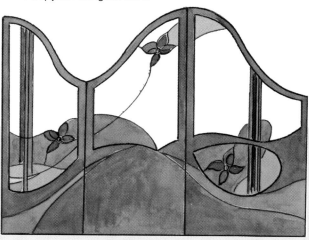

Designs are shown in the space they will inhabit. Design by Julia Rodríguez of a panel set in a wall tiled with modernist tiles and lit from behind. Ink and gouache on paper, 2005.

Creating models

Creating three dimensional works can require the creation of maquettes. These can range from simple models to very detailed maquettes. In the maquettes the design is given a three dimensional form. The artist gets close to how the work will look, resolving and eliminating possible problems of the plan and ensuring that the final work adheres to the original design. The creation of some objects, such as lampshades, require the creation of molds. In general, these are made on a support made of Porexpan, which allows the design to be fully expressed, as a model for the piece and for the cut templates and as support or mold for the assembly.

1 For the design and creation of a shade pieces of Porexpan are used. Here, a sphere has been cut in half to create a semi-sphere.

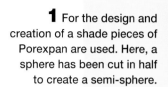

2 To mark out the parts of the shade the inner circumference of the piece is divided with the help of a compass. The divisions are marked out with a permanent marker.

3 Next, the lines are extended until the central point of the semi-sphere and the design is shown with a marker pen.

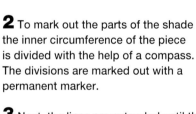

4 and **5** The molds can reflect the complete design of the shade, as in the first example, or just one of the parts, which is repeated until it makes up the whole circumference.

Making templates

Flat templates

Once the design is complete different templates are made which serve as a guide for cutting the glass and assembling the pieces. First a scale drawing is created which will define the metal framework and the mosaic of pieces of glass which will make up the piece; this is usually done on white kraft paper. In general the designs are executed on a 1:5 or 1:10 scale, whilst the life size drawing is on a 1:1 scale. In this the shapes of the pieces and the joint lines are shown and then they are used to develop the template to cut the glass and act as a guide during the assembly. This drawing is also useful for assessing the suitability of the design, that is, to see that there are no unfinished lines, pieces that require difficult cuts (very sharp points, narrow areas or very close curves that could lead to the glass breaking) or areas with too many convergences of joining lines, for example. Once the drawing is done to scale, the template for the pieces is made by tracing onto natural color kraft paper; for this each piece is marked with a number and then cut with stained glass pattern shears.

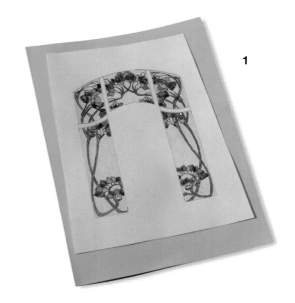

1 The templates are made from the design, in this case a plan for the side panels of a door, a reproduction of a modernist window by Julia Rodríguez, made in 2007 to 1:10 scale, that is each centimetre of the plan is equivalent to 10 cm of the real piece.

2 As this is an object made of five pieces which will be fixed on to an existing structure, different drawing are executed. One drawing is made for the two upper side parts, which are symmetrical, the layout of the pattern is marked and the lines traced over with pencil. The process is repeated, making one drawing for the two lower side parts, which are also symmetrical and lastly the drawing of the central part.

3 The drawing is placed on a sheet of natural colored craft paper, with carbon paper in between them, and it is held in place with masking tape, drawing pins or nails. The pattern is traced by going over the lines in pencil or biro, and each piece is numbered.

4 The result is a tracing of the original drawing where the shapes appear with the same number on them.

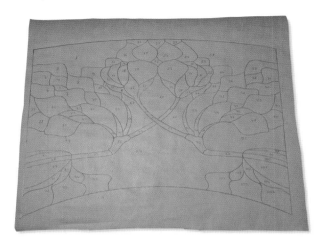

4

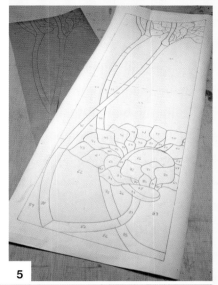

5

5 The same process is carried out for the drawing of the lower side part. To create symmetrical parts (upper and lower side parts) just the original drawing and a template made by tracing are used; two identical pieces of glass are cut with each template taking into account the symmetry in the case of the textured glass and the assembly of one piece is done on the front and of the other on the back of the drawing.

6 The shapes are cut with stained glass pattern shears, in this case, for copper. The cutting is carried out carefully, following the lines of the central part and ensuring that they are continuous.

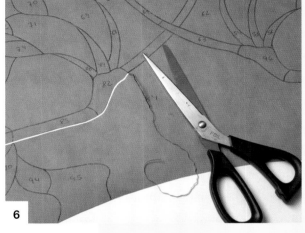

6

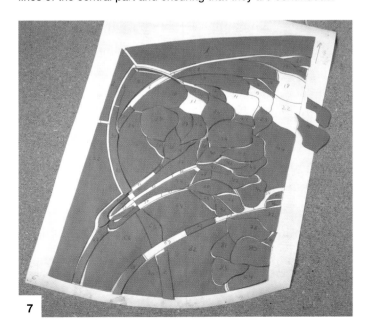

7

7 As the templates are cut out they are laid out on the drawing, to check that they fit and that there are none missing.

8 The templates serve as a guide for cutting the glass. Once cut, the pieces are laid out on a tray, arranged together with the corresponding templates, in order to facilitate assembly.

9 The scale drawing acts as a guide for the pieces of glass, which are laid out on it in order to check that they fit and that none are missing.

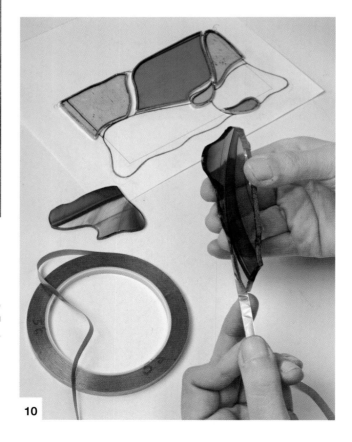

10 It also serves as a guide during the assembly process, both for leaded pieces and those made with copper foil technique.

Templates for shapes with volume

The creation of three dimensional works requires a particular process to make templates. Once the three dimensional mold is made (a lampshade for example), templates for each piece are made separately by tracing directly from the mold.

To do this, each of the pieces which make up the original, or in some cases a single piece, are traced in pencil onto tracing paper, and are numbered. After making the tracing of the pieces they are cut out with stained glass pattern shears for copper and the glass is cut using them as a guide. Assembly of the pieces is done on the mold, as in the step by step example given for the floor lamp (see page 108).

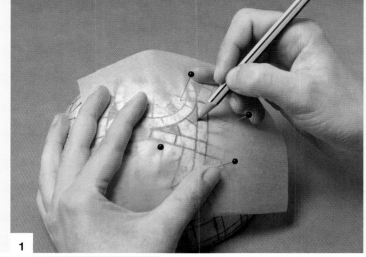

1

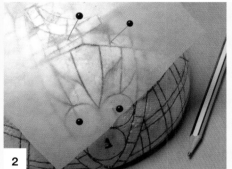

2

1 The tracing paper is fixed onto the mold with some pins and then the lines are traced in pencil. The patterns on the same piece are traced, that is, those which are under the paper, and they are numbered.

2 The large pieces which occupy a whole piece are traced separately.

3 All the shapes of the templates are numbered, they are also numbered on the mold, which will act as a guide for assembly.

4 The finished lampshade once assembled.

3

4

CUTTING AND POLISHING GLASS

Cutting is the fundamental aspect which anyone who wants to work with glass must master. Glass has very defined characteristics which make it appear like a solid mass. Breaks or fractures are produced by traction when it reaches the limits of its resistance. Cutting is, in fact, a fracture, a mark on the glass which produces a line of weakness, which can have pressure applied to it or be tapped in order to cause the material to be fractured.

Types of **cuts**

Prior considerations

The use of different types of glass offers great possiblilities for artistic forms which are worth assessing before starting the cutting process. By doing this, the characteristics of the glass can help to emphasize the design and create particular effects. On the other hand, using some varieties of glass whose characteristics do not fit with the design can result in artworks which are uninteresting or even unpleasant to look at. Favrile glass is an interesting area, as depending on how the cutting is carried out, it allows for pieces to be created where the washes in the color become visual elements in the composition. The possibilities are infinite, as it is also possible to create effects combining glass of different textures and surfaces such as textured glass, as well as molded glass and even others with special characteristics such as iridescent or opalescent glass.

In this example a decorative panel for a house has been made depicting a seabird. To recreate the effects of the sea Favrile glass in greeny tones with blues washes has been used; it is cut so that the visual effect of the blue emphasizes the wavy shapes of the design.

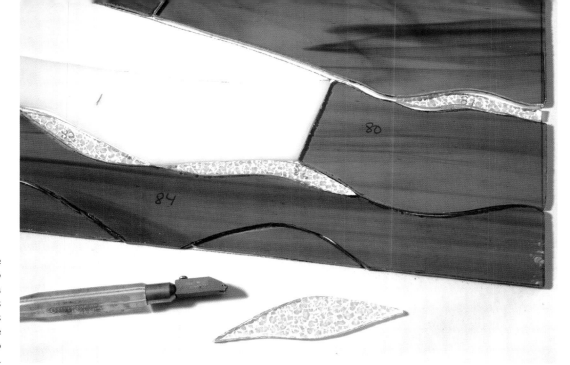

In the same example, to recreate the sea foam, colorless textured glass has been used for the details on the top of the waves.

Straight cut

Cutting glass is not a particularly difficult task, although it requires a little skill and some prior practice to make precise cuts. It is advisable to bear in mind that any cutting work must be perfectly planned otherwise part of the material could be wasted. The cutting is done by marking the glass with the cutter, putting pressure on it and moving it towards the person cutting: this gives a line of weakness which will fracture when pressure is put on it or it is hit at the bottom end. Any kind of textured glass is marked on the smooth side. All cutting is carried out on a cutting table, a high strong table which allows work to be carried out whilst standing; it should have a firm and soft surface (wood or felt covered chipboard).

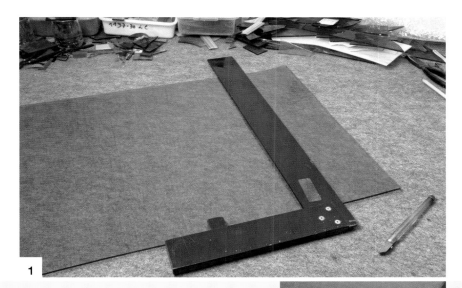

1

1 First the glass is measured out to the desired size and the glass cutter's square is placed on it; this should be large enough to cover the whole cutting line. The smaller arm is placed next to the lower edge of the glass and the larger arm set to the desired measurement.

2 To place the square as a guide for the cutting line the millimetres which separate the cutter from the side edge of the head (in this case 2.5mm) are added, then the cut is carried out.

2

3 Fix the square firmly onto the glass by pressing down with one hand, whilst using the other for the cutter. Place this on the glass, without pressing down too hard on it, using the square as a guide. The cut must go from the end of the line towards the person cutting. Do not go over it twice.

4 Once the line of weakness has been drawn it can be difficult to see. Next, the glass is broken by "opening" it. Tap softly under the line with the handle or head of the cutter until the cut appears.

3

4

5

5 Next, open the glass by hand; to do this hold the glass on one side, slightly raised off the cutting table, and then push upwards with fingers placed on either side of the line.

Circular and curved cuts

Circular and curved cuts, that is, cutting circles, inner or concave curves of wavy shapes, require more complex processes than cutting shapes with straight edges. Cutting is carried out in various phases, removing the leftover glass by means of successive cuts until the desired shape is achieved. There are different methods for these cuts. For cutting circular pieces the most usual way is to use the beam compass to mark the line of weakness, although circles can also be achieved by carrying out a series of tangent cuts (to 45°) to the line of the shape and then sharpening it up afterwards with pincers.

CUTTING A CIRCLE

Circle cutting is done with a beam compass or cutting compass, a tool which is easy to use and does not differ from an ordinary compass. This tool needs to be used with lubricating oil to facilitate the marking of the line of weakness on the glass. Once the line has been done and opened by tapping, the glass is marked from the central circle towards the outside to indicate the lines with which the surrounding glass will be broken into pieces.

1 Place the compass in the chosen place with the sucker on the exact spot, and close the screw. Put the cutting point with the handle at the desired measurement according to the marks on the compass arm and apply a drop of lubricant oil onto the cutting point. Hold the glass by hand and move the arm of the compass by holding the handle of the cutting point with the other hand without pressing down.

2 Open by breaking the circle cut, tapping lightly under the line of weakness with the head of the cutter.

1

2

3 To remove the leftover glass, make a line of weakness on each side; starting from the circle line and moving the cutter towards the outside

3

4 Open the lines with a soft tap on the lower part by using the metal head of a cutter to produce the fracture.

5 The circular piece and the side pieces once the cutting process is finished.

4

5

CUTTING INSIDE CURVES

Cutting shapes which have some curves towards the inside of the glass is not difficult, although it requires a longer process than that for circular pieces and involves a greater number of steps. Due to the complexity of the shape it is necessary to make multiple weakness lines, removing the leftover glass in phases. Concave shapes can be made by two different methods which are explained here.

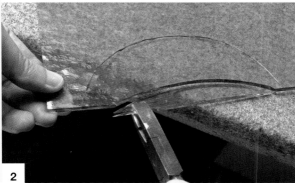

1 To make shapes curved towards the inside of the glass, first mark the line of weakness of the final shape and open by lightly tapping with the head of the cutter on the bottom of t he glass.

2 Remove the glass inside by making successive cuts from the outside to the inside. First mark an outside line with a soft curve and break the glass with the aid of pliers.

3 Keep making successive cuts, as if they were segments, increasing the curvature of the pieces until the final shape is achieved

Another method for achieving concave curves is the following: once the desired line of the shape is marked and opened, use a cutter to make a series of straight lines inside the shape, then fracture the glass tapping lightly down these lines removing the pieces until the desired shape is achieved.

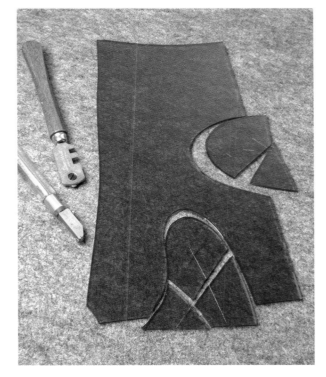

WAVY CUTS

To make wavy cuts, first draw the line of weakness and then open it by means of soft taps or by pressure. These cuts require the cutter to be used correctly; also they must be continuous and not repeated. In all cases, the line of weakness is continued to the end of the glass to remove the leftover glass more efficiently. On the pieces with various wavy shapes all the various lines are also marked until the end of the glass.

To make wavy cuts extend the line until the end of the piece of glass, then open it by tapping it lightly with head of a cutter.

1

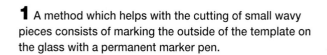

1 A method which helps with the cutting of small wavy pieces consists of marking the outside of the template on the glass with a permanent marker pen.

2 Next, mark the line of weakness, going over it with a cutter and continuing the line until the edge of the glass. In this case, the cuts are opened with pliers. However, this method is less precise than cutting directly with the template.

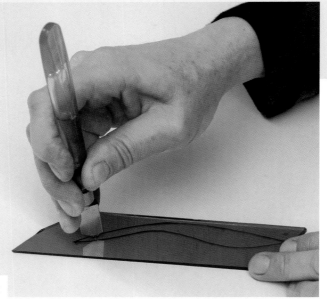

2

Smoothing

Cut pieces or shapes can have barbs, that is, small bits of glass that protrude unevenly from the edge of the glass. To finish off the line or shape of the cut properly it is necessary to remove all possible barbs, smoothing them with the help of pliers. Using the tip of the pliers, make small pinches to remove the leftover glass or use the back to scrape and get rid of imperfections.

1

1 When it is broken, the glass can have barbs which must be removed before the work is assembled.

2 The small barbs are removed by going over the glass carefully with the back of the pliers.

2

3

3 Barbs which are very visible are removed by making small pinches with the pliers, hold the material firmly so to be able to turn the tool slightly, taking care not to apply too much pressure as this can cause breaks.

Basic techniques

Polishing

To smooth the surface of the cuts the edges of the cut pieces are polished. Polishing is an easy and quick process carried out with a side polisher, which can also be used to make shapes.
This process is essential when making objects with copper foil technique. Polishing the cut results in a porous surface which allows the adhesive on the back of the copper foil to hold the glass more easily, ensuring the copper sticks correctly. To polish, place the glass on the grid base or mesh of the machine and touch the pieces to the fast rotating grindstone.

To polish the edges of the cut pieces use the edge polisher. When the pieces touch the grindstone it polishes the edges. The glass must be held on the opposite edge to the grindstone.

1 Before assembling pieces with the copper foil technique it is essential to polish all their sides.

2 Doing this means the cut has a porous surface which ensures the copper foil, which serves as a support for the subsequent soldering, sticks properly.

Shaping

The shaping polisher also allows for the shaping of pieces, it allows the desired shape to be achieved by grinding down the edge or the surface of the glass. The polisher wears away the glass until the desired shape is obtained. This process is very suitable for small pieces with very pronounced wavy edges which cannot be cut with a cutter, as they may break, or when the pieces have to be adjusted during assembly to remove a small part of the glass.

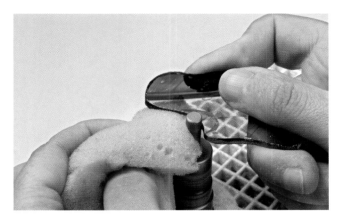

To shape small pieces with very pronounced wavy shapes the polisher is used. Mark the desired shape with wax pencil on glass and touch it to the high speed grindstone to wear the glass down. The pressure put on the glass has to be carefully controlled so as not to wear the glass down too much.

1 When assembling pieces for leaded glass it may be necessary to make small adjustments to some pieces of glass. Once set down the piece corresponds to the real measurements of the template, it can be seen that the one or other of the side is slightly bigger than the template.
Take the lead as a reference and mark the edge with a permanent marker with a fine tip.

1

2 Use the polisher on the edge and remove the excess glass, wearing it away with the grindstone until the mark is reached.

2

GLASSWORK

The creation of glassworks with lead and copper foil is not limited to making pieces by joining glass of different types; it is also possible to work on the glass beforehand in the studio. This work offers an unlimited range of possibilities by varying the color with painting in grisaille, silver stain and enamels or texture by finishing it with sandblasting. In these works, the light is converted into another aspect of the composition, as in most cases the characteristics of the glass are appreciated for their transparent appearance.

Grisaille

Preparation

Grisaille, like enamel, is applied, mixed with a vehicle, onto glass as a painting paste. It comes in powder form, therefore it needs prior preparation which can be used with different vehicles (distilled water, vinegar, turpentine, essence of turpentine, ox gall or alcohol) and by adding different elements as binders (gum arabic, sugar or shellac) or fluidizers (glycerine), depending on the use required.

The paint paste is applied as if it were paint, bearing in mind that glass does not have a porous surface, it is then dried and fired in the kiln. Like paint, grisaille can be worked in coats, first by making an outline, then the wash and finally the shape. The coats can be applied one on top of the other once dry and with a final firing or firing between each one. In the first case, when working with coats and a final firing, a different

vehicle is used for each one. In general, vinegar is used with the paint for the outline, water for the wash and essence of turpentine for the second wash or filling in. In the second case when a firing is done after each coat, the same vehicle can be used. When used as a binder, gum arabic can only be mixed with vinegar and water.

1 To prepare the grisaille painting paste put the estimated amount needed onto a glass support and use it like a palette and then add drops of vinegar.

2 Mix it with a palette knife, stirring until an even paste is achieved with the liquid consistency of paint.

Outlining

The first stage of painting with grisaille is outlining, also called threading, transferring the lines of the pattern onto the glass; usually this is done in black or brown grisaille. It is applied to the glass placed on a template or sketch with the lines of the work which is on top of a light box. This box can be substituted by a piece of tempered frosted glass held by an easel and some daylight fluorescent lights. The outlining can be done with vinegar as the vehicle, adding two drops of gum arabic or with distilled water. If any mistakes are made they can be corrected; allow the painting paste to dry and then scratch with a knife to remove the grisaille.

1 Apply the grisaille onto the glass (matt in this case) which is completely clean and free of grease. Place it on the template (here, a design inspired by Arabic designs) and outline the lines in black grisaille with a thin soft-haired rounded paintbrush. For very precise details use a fountain pen.

2 The main pattern, once finished, corresponds to the template. Leave it to dry.

3 Next, put it inside the kiln and leave it for a firing cycle with a slow temperature rise from room temperature up to 600 °C in 20 minutes. Turn the kiln off and let the inside cool down until it reaches room temperature. For larger pieces the rising temperature should be increased.

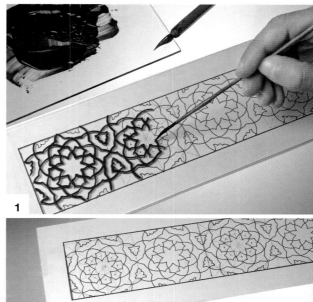

1

2

3

Wash

The wash is a color glaze of medium intensity which is applied on top of the outline and makes up the first coat of color for the piece. It acts as a transition between the darker parts of the paint and the lighter ones. It is a color paste more liquid than that used for outlining, and it is applied with a soft-haired wide paintbrush with generous brushstrokes and when, still wet, is spread with a soft-haired wide brush to create an even surface. Once dry, the color coat can be removed in some places to create transparent or areas which are translucent to the light.

1 Once the previous outline has been filled, prepare a light brown grisaille using water as a vehicle until a liquid painting paste is achieved. Apply this onto the pattern with generous brushstrokes with a wide soft-haired brush.

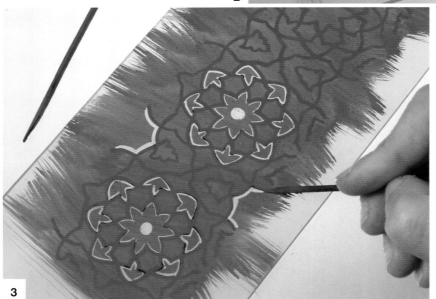

2 Without waiting for the paste to dry spread it with a soft-haired brush (in this case badger hair) with up and down, right to left and diagonal movements until an even surface is achieved. Then let it dry.

3 Removing the color in particular areas allows for transparent visible effects to be created. Outline the flower with the central circle, the patterns around it and the outside shapes, taking the color off with a wooden stick.

4 To spread the color over a wider area (inside the palm shapes and to create the circles around the flowers), a short-haired bristle brush can be used.

5 Tapping softly with the pitua brush take off part of the paint in some areas, creating a textured effect. To finish, it is fired in a similar process to the previous firing.

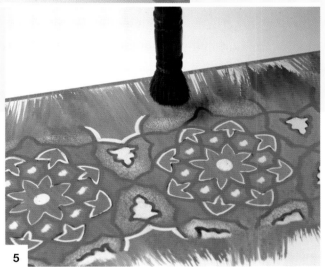

6 Once the firing is carried out, to see the light effects achieved take off the grisaille, working the paste whilst dry. With firing, the tone of the grisaille becomes less intense.

Shaping

Shaping is done by the application of successive coats of glaze working each of them whilst dry to achieve light effects which give an appearance of tonal grading. A coat of glaze is applied onto the previously glazed piece, putting the liquid paste on with a wide soft-haired paintbrush and spreading it with a wide soft brush to create an even surface. To create the effects of shaping the grisaille can be worked dry with pins or different tips to create small details, short-haired bristle brushes can be used to remove the grisaille in certain areas, paintbrushes used to create areas with brushstroke effects, soft haired pitua brushes can create dotting or textured effects and even two fingers can be used. The selective removal layer by layer will allow for the effects of shaping, creating different forms. Once the shaping is finished and the piece is fired some effects can be added with enamels or silver stain.

1 Apply a glaze of liquid grisaille prepared with distilled water with a soft-haired paintbrush. Then without waiting for it to dry, spread it with a badger hair brush to create an even surface and let it dry.

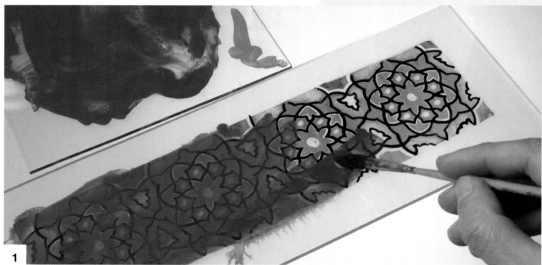

2 Work on the piece by taking the glaze off in some areas: outline with a stick on the outlined areas in wash, take off the coat on the palm shapes and other elements with wash by using a short-haired bristle brush and work other areas creating texture with the pitua brush.

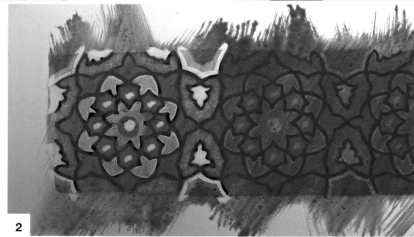

3 The details of the circle and the palm shapes are painted with blue enamel, which contrasts vividly with the light brown grisaille glazes. Next put it in the kiln for a firing cycle with a slow rise from room temperature to 600 °C in 20 minutes, turn the kiln off and let it cool inside until it reaches room temperature.

4 In the finished piece the effects of the shaping created by the successive coats of grisaille can be seen as well as the different lights.

The grisaille can also be used to outline pieces which, once glazed, are colored with enamels.

Silver stain

Silver stain is prepared in the same way as grisaille, mixing with water and blending until a thick even painting paste is achieved. It is also applied with a wide soft-haired paintbrush and spread before drying with a soft haired brush to create an even surface. It is worked over a light table like the grisaille. Silver stain combined with the previously fired grisaille gives interesting effects on the glass, where all the deep yellow and transparent silver stain yellows contrast in color and with the opacity of the grisaille. The pieces with silver stain applied to them are put in the kiln with the painted face upwards, as they must not touch the ceramic fibre used as a base in the kiln. However, there is no problem with the grisaille coming into contact with the fibre during the firing. Once the firing cycle is finished and the glass is at room temperature, it is possible to recover the leftover silver stain to be reused by scraping the surface with a hard-haired paintbrush.

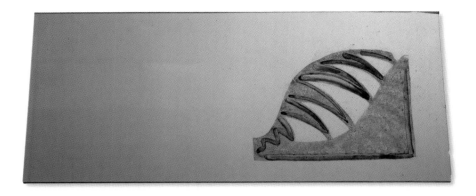

1 Silver stain work on a manufactured smooth amber colored glass previously worked with grisaille

2 Once the silver stain is prepared it is applied to the glass with a soft-haired paintbrush. The inside areas of the shape and the top part of the square are painted with grisaille.

3 Without waiting for it to dry, used the pitua brush or a very soft-haired wide paintbrush (in this case badger hair) to spread the paste upwards, from left to right and diagonally until an even surface is obtained. Then leave it to dry.

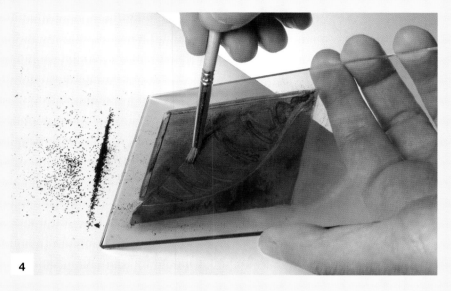

4 Place it in the kiln with the painted side upwards and leave it for a firing cycle with a rise from room temperature to 600 °C in 20 minutes, turn the kiln off and leave it to cool inside until it is at room temperature. Next, scrape the surface with a short-haired bristle brush to remove the leftover silver stain, and put the resulting powder onto a clean piece of paper to collect it and return it to its container.

5 The cleaned and finished piece.

6 Depending on the thickness of the layer of painting paste applied on the glass, different ranges of tone are achieved from deep yellow to amber.

Enamels

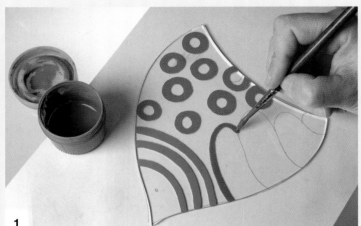

Enamels, just like grisaille and silver stain, are prepared by mixing with distilled water and stirring until an even paste is achieved, neither too thick nor too liquid; then they are applied to glass over a light table. In general opaque enamels are the most suitable for outlining and transparent enamels are used for coloring areas of the glass, although it depends on the aesthetic components of each work. Enamels cannot be mixed to obtain a tone or color as if they were paints, but coats are applied to achieve the desired color effect. That is, a coat is applied, left to dry and then put in the kiln for a firing cycle similar to that explained in the previous section; afterwards a second coat is applied and then it is fired again and so on. Opaque enamels can be worked by removing the layer of paint in a similar way to grisaille, creating areas of light which contrast when lit from behind with the surrounding opaque areas.

1 In this example the body of a fish is being made for a mobile. Use a colorless manufactured glass already cut with a template on top of a light table and outline the main shapes with opaque enamels in blue, red and green. Leave to dry and fire in a similar way to the example in the previous section.

2 Fill in the shapes with light green, yellow and purple transparent enamels, and also outline the red circles in orange opaque enamel and stipple the background with opaque white enamel.

3 Carry out a second firing cycle similar to the previous one. Appearance of the enamel once finished.

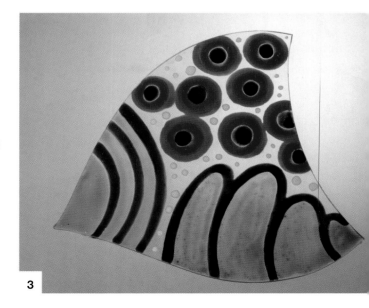

1 Opaque enamel offers other possibilities apart from outlining. Here, an opal glass is being painted with blue enamel to make a candle holder. It is painted with brushstrokes which make wavy lines like waves and then it is left to dry.

2 When the enamel is dry, the brushstrokes are visible, and will be more pronounced after firing.

3 To create light effects, take off the enamel with the help of a thin wooden stick. Next, carry out a firing cycle similar to the previous one.

4 The opaque enamel of this candle holder made with the copper foil technique is applied with wavy brushstrokes and then worked by removing the enamel with a pin to achieve very fine lines.

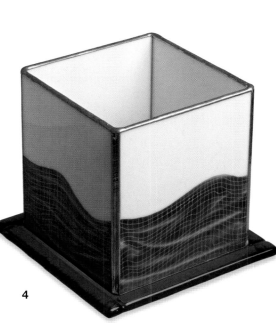

Basic techniques

Sandblasting

With sandblasting it is possible to create translucent and matt surfaces that contrast vividly with the transparent and shiny surface of the unworked glass, creating very interesting visual effects which help to give depth to the work. The work is designed and shields are made to protect the areas which are to be safeguarded form the action of the sandblaster. The shields can be in positive or negative, that is, protecting the design and leaving the background matt or protecting the background and leaving the pattern to be worked respectively. To make the shields usually sheets of sticky back plastic, white glue or latex are used. These last two are applied directly on to the glass with a paintbrush, allowing for freer shapes than those achieved with plastic and paintbrushes.

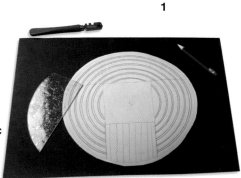

1 In this example, a shield is made with a sheet of sticky back plastic on a sheet of colorless antique glass which will form part of a sculpture. First draw the part of the pattern which is to be protected on paper, in this case, six lines on each of the sides and upper panels making up the work.

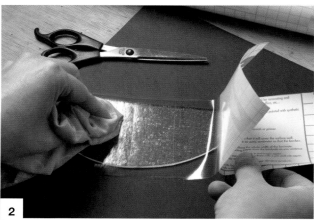

2 Fix the sheet of sticky back plastic onto the surface to be worked by rubbing it with a clean cloth to remove any bubbles.

3 It is possible to make shields in different ways; one of these is to trace the shapes of the pattern of the template onto the sticky back plastic with a permanent marker pen and then cut. It is also possible to make the cuts directly, using the template as a guide. Follow the lines of the template with a cutter which will cut the plastic cleanly.

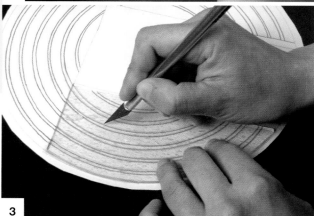

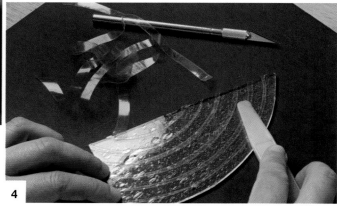

4 Remove the leftover plastic covering the parts which will be worked on with the sandblaster and ensure that the shields are stuck by using the lead knife.

SANDBLASTING GLASS

Blasting is the result of the surface abrasion of glass with a solid abrasive blasted at high pressure resulting in translucent and matt surfaces similar to those achieved with acid cream. This technique, however, allows for more elaborate finishes as it is possible to achieve different degrees of matt effects and even to cut glass. A certain amount of practice is needed before starting work so it is advisable to do some tests on pieces of glass varying the time and pressure. The pistol must be moved continuously, never less than 7cm away from the surface of the glass, in circular movements, or alternating vertical and horizontal movements (which should finish off the glass) and continuous movements to avoid the abrasion being bigger in some parts than others.

1 Sandblast the glass by vertical and horizontal movements and check the progress of the work and the state and adhesion of the shields regularly. It is advisable to wear specialized protective gear; thick gloves and an anti dust mask.

2 Take out the glass and remove the power deposited on the piece with a cloth and then take off the shields.

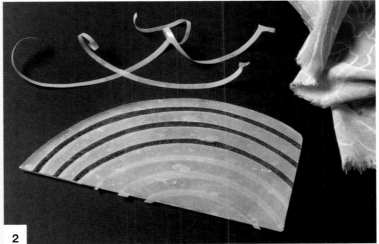

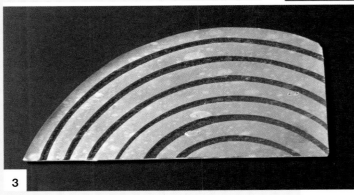

3 Clean the glass with water and detergent and then dry it. The protected lines contrast with the matt background. Note that the surface abrasion has caused the surface breakage of some of the barbs of this piece of glass.

GRINDING FLASHED GLASS

One of the most interesting possibilities offered by this technique is with flashed glass. With the sandblasting the colored layer of the glass can be removed, grinding it down or eliminating it completely in some areas to create some effects such as tonal grading, or so that the shielded areas (which will then appear in their original color) contrast volume, color range and visually with respect to the background. The creation of shields and the use of the blasting machine is similar to that explained previously. Next, the method for blasting flashed glass and the creation of shields with white glue are shown.

1

2

1 The flashed glass worked on here is made of one colorless and one red layer. First do a sketch of the pattern in pencil on paper.

2 With the sketch as a guide paint the patterns on the surface with the red layer with white glue and let it dry.

3 Blast the glass in the sandblasting machine, working it to create a background with uneven shading.

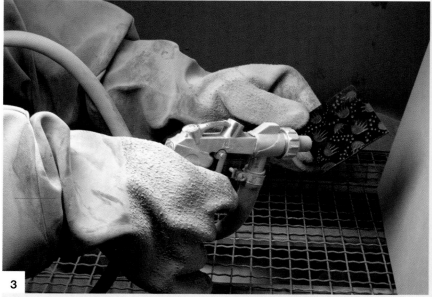

3

4 The shielded areas have been protected by the white glue. The background has been made matt in an unequal manner, giving room for different degrees of shading.

5 Clean the glass in a container with running water and remove the shields by rubbing with a soft synthetic brush, in this case a toothbrush.

6 and **7** The result is a piece where the patterns of colored glass and the smooth and shiny surface stand out from the matt background with shading. Looking at the glass when lit from above and held up to the light brings out the effects of the piece.

LEADING

Leading consists of assembling a piece by joining the pieces of glass with strips of lead or lead came. It is done from a life size drawing (see page 34) usually done on white paper and on a table specifically for assembly. This is a large table, high enough to be able to work standing up, with a strong wooden top onto which tacks and nails used for holding the pieces during the leading process can be nailed. Once the work is completed it is essential to wash your hands to avoid any possible toxic effects from the material.

Basic aspects

Starting and holding the elements in place

Once the drawing is fixed onto the assembly table (masking tape or nails can be used) place the initial element of the work in the desired position. This element, depending on the object being made, can be one of the lead cames which makes up a side of the composition or the largest or main piece of glass. Before starting any work it is advisable to establish the order of the steps involved. After placing the initial piece, fix it correctly with tacks or nails on the table to avoid any possible movement during the assembly. In addition, to avoid possible distortion, fix the lead came by inserting a piece of glass between it and the nail or tack situated inside the wings of the rod. The glass for assembly is held by inserting a fragment of lead between it and the nail, or directly with the tacks.

Here, the underside of the lead came is situated according to its layout in the drawing and it is held in place with a piece of glass which spans its length. For large strips of lead use a small piece of glass for each nail.

To hold the glass before starting the assembly insert a small fragment of lead between the glass and the nail.

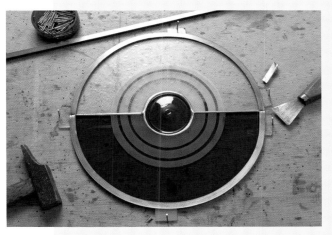

It is also possible to hold the glass in place with tacks. These are nailed onto the assembly table, slightly leaning outwards, as if they are nailed inwards they might raise the glass and cause it to come loose or break.

As the assembly take place secure the lead cames. In this case, they need a few fixing points and the joint of the lead on the left is done with a single nail by a glass which spans both pieces.

During the assembly, the pieces of glass are held in place with nails or tacks by inserting a fragment of lead strip.

Fixing in this way ensures that each element stays in the right place during the assembly. Here, to fix the two petals of the flowers a piece of glass (yellow) which is alongside is used and it has been fixed with a single nail.

Assembly

Once the main piece is placed then assembly begins. This work is done in stages and in order, fitting the lead cames and the pieces of glass in such a way that each piece added to the whole is supported by the pieces already assembled, avoiding any holes. Continue in order, from the main piece until the end without leaving any gaps to assemble. If this were to happen, the elements would not fit together correctly and it would not be possible to place them in the layout marked on the template.

PLACING THE PIECES OF GLASS

The pieces of glass fit into the heart of the lead cames, in between the wings. To ensure the correct fit tap the side of the cut lightly with the handle of the hammer, a stick with a rubber or nylon head or directly with the hammer inserting a wooden plug. Once placed these are fixed with nails or tacks to avoid them coming loose. To ensure the correct join with the other pieces of lead, next, tap the end of the lead came, and remove the leftover part by separating it with the cutting knife. Then flatten the end by hitting with the hammer.

1 The piece of glass is situated in such a way that it fits in the heart of the lead came, between the wings, and stays according to the layout marked on the drawing fixed on the assembly table.

2 To ensure that it fits into the lead, push it in by tapping the side of the piece gently, with the handle of the hammer, until it is all in.

3 The piece must coincide with the shape marked on the drawing. Fix it by driving in a tack or a nail, inserting a fragment of lead to avoid damage to the glass.

4 Next, finish off the shape by encircling it with the lead on the left (see the previous image); for this, it is necessary to remove the leftover part of the vertical lead came. Using the drawing as a reference, mark the ends of the cuts by pressing down with the lead knife.

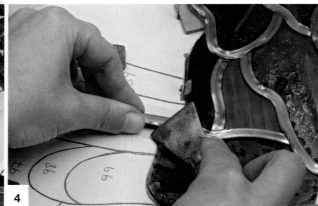

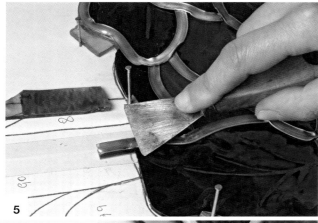

5

6

7

5 To cut, place the cutting knife perpendicular to the lead came, at a right angle, following the line of the drawing and previous mark.

6 The cut is produced when pressing down at the same time as moving the knife from side to side. The blade must be very well-sharpened, otherwise instead of cutting the lead it will only squash it.

7 The result is the clean cut of the lead according to the shapes of the original drawing.

8 Flatten the end of the lead where it has been cut by placing the lead knife underneath all of it and tapping softly with the hammer. The knife acts as a wedge making it easier for the underside of the lead to be slightly raised, thus facilitating the fit.

8

PLACING THE LEAD CAMES

Before placing the lead cames they have to be stretched. For this, it is practical to use a vise fixed to the work table: trapping a piece of the lead in it, pull the other by hand until the lead is as straight as possible. If a vise is not used, hold one end on the floor firmly by the heel of your foot and pull the other end. During this process the wings tend to pull together, so that before placing it near the pieces of glass it is essential to separate these by passing the lead knife along the heart on both sides of the strip. The joints between the lead cames are made by fitting one lead inside the other; raise the joint area of the lead which is on the outside and insert the end of the other piece of lead under its wings.

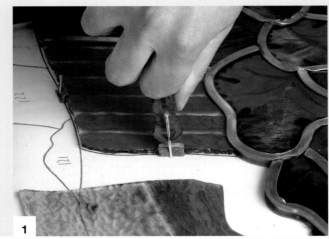

1 Remove the nail that is fixing the piece on the side where the lead is going to be placed, and leave the other one to avoid problems of faults in the glass. Always follow this process, only remove the necessary nails or tacks to be able to place each lead came and leave the others to ensure the correct fit of the pieces.

2 Place the lead on the piece and mark the cutting line with the lead knife, leaving the piece a little longer than necessary. Then, cut it as in the previous section.

3 Separate the wings of both sides of the lead came by passing the curved end of the lead knife (the "bird" knife) along the heart.

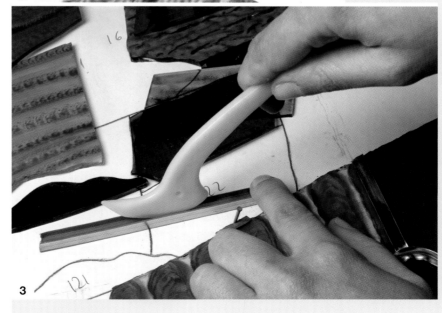

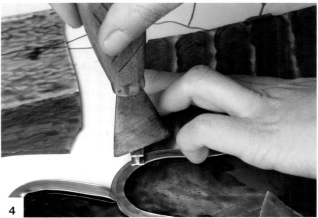

4 The end of the lead came which is inserted into the inside of the lead of the piece situated on the lower side is cut with the angle determined by the previous piece. For this, place it according to the layout of the lead it will fit into and mark the cutting line. Then cut it on the table with the cutting knife.

5 To make it fit lift the wing of the lead came up with the tip of the knife blade.

6 Insert the lead came inside the wings of the other lead, paying special attention to keeping the piece of glass in the heart.

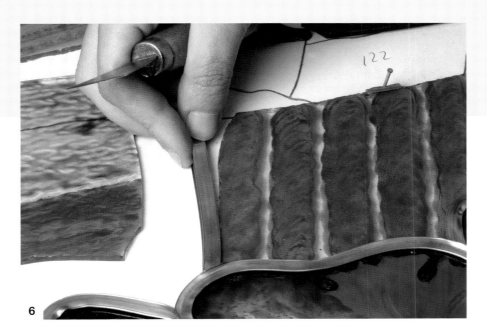

Basic techniques

To place the lead came the curved lead knife (also called "bird" knife) can be used, pressing the heart of the strip with the flat end. To facilitate the work, lift the glass slightly and insert the curved cutting knife between it and the cutting table.

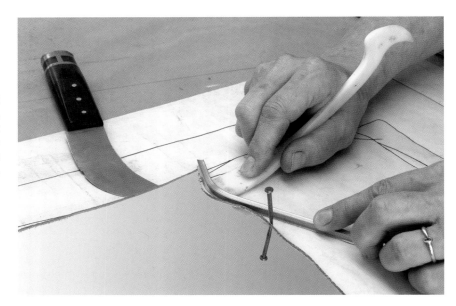

Once the lead is placed in the correct layout, hold it with the glass and a tack: next, continue placing the lead in the rest of the piece and hold in this way when necessary.

The pieces can be shaped by curving a single piece of lead.

FLATTENING THE LEADS

Once the assembly of the work is finished then the wings of the lead came are flattened. This means that the wings are squashed down trapping the pieces of glass, helping it to be secured, at the same time as the outside surface of the lead cames on the top or side of the piece are rounded.

Flatten the wings of the lead cames by pressing down with the end of the lead knife, on either side of the lead came. The result is the rounded surface of the strips.

The lead cutting knife can also be used. In this case, proceed carefully to avoid marking the lead.

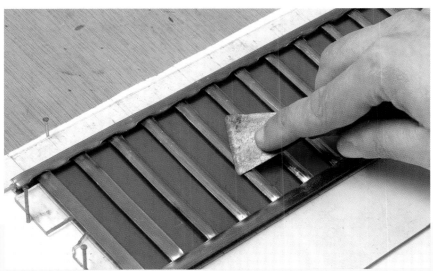

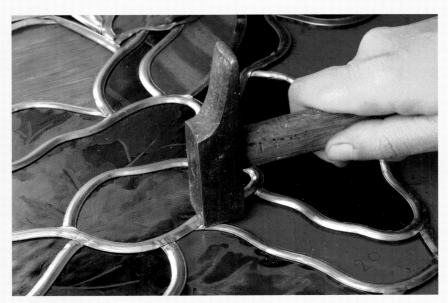

Lastly, tap the joints of the lead with the hammer to flatten the surface of the solder.

Soldering

Once the assembly is complete the joints of the lead cames are soldered. Although this needs some practice, it is a quick and relatively easy process. After applying the flux for lead which is composed of estearin on the soldering points, apply solder (an alloy of 50% solder and 50% lead); to do this, move the end of the rod and the soldering iron to the point of the joint and press lightly with it on the lead for a few seconds. The amount of flux and solder is controlled to avoid incorrect soldering or excessive accumulation of material. The soldering should be firm, smooth and flat. The work is first done on one side of the piece and then the other side is soldered. Before beginning the soldering it is essential to check that the solder is at the right temperature, making sure that it melts. However, it is even more important to make certain that it is not too hot, as it could melt the lead.

Before starting check the temperature of the tip of the soldering iron to avoid the lead melting. To do this, do a test on a fragment of lead with a small amount of solder. If the solder is too hot it will melt the lead quickly.

1

1 To solder apply stearin flux onto the lead joints.

2 Place the rod of solder and the soldering iron onto the point and melt the solder, moving it onto the lead came with the tip of the soldering iron.

2

3 Press lightly onto the lead with the tip of the soldering iron.

3

Applying putty and cleaning

Applying putty consists of making the putty penetrate the gaps between the pieces of glass and the wings of the lead came ensuring they stay firmly fixed together. This helps to make the work robust, securing the glass to the lead and waterproofing the joints. Once the soldering is done on one side, turn the work over and continue to solder the other side without flattening the lead cames (only close the surface of the soldering) and apply putty with the help of a esparto grass brush, ensuring that it penetrates under the wings of the lead; next, flatten the lead cames and remove the excess with sawdust. Leave to dry for 36 to 48 hours, after which remove the dry residue left on the glass (corners and other difficult to reach areas) with the tip of a stick or wooden rod.

1 Once the soldering has been done on one side, turn the work over and continue to solder the joints of the lead cames before applying putty.

2 Apply the putty with an esparto grass brush using circular movements, making sure that it penetrates between the lead and the glass.

3 To remove the leftover putty sprinkle sawdust by hand, using gloves. Then with the help of a brush, press it into the corners and collect the excess sawdust.

Basic techniques

COPPER FOIL TECHNIQUE

This technique was developed by Louis Comfort Tiffany at the end of the 19th century. In essence it consists of using copper foil as the base of the solder which joins all the sides of the work in place of lead. It allows for lighter, less rigid works, as well as joint lines that are thinner than lead. It also allows for work with curved surfaces to be created as well as for small pieces of glass to be used.

Basic aspects

Edging

When the preparatory process (creation of the design and templates) is done and the cutting of all the pieces of glass which make up the work, the edges of the cuts are polished, that is the outside, with the edge polisher. The polishing gives a porous surface which allows for the copper foil to stick properly. This aspect is fundamental, as the foil acts as a base for the soldering and if it comes off this can cause problems. Once the pieces are polished it is essential to clean them with a clean cloth to remove any particles and remains of the dust which can make it difficult for the copper foil to stick correctly. This is stuck onto the outside of each piece of glass in such a way that the edge of the glass is always in the middle of the foil. This must cover 1mm of each surface side of the glass, and therefore it is necessary to use a foil with the right width for each thickness of glass.

1

1 Polish the cut edges of the glass to achieve a porous surface and clean them with a cloth to remove any particles. Choose a copper foil that corresponds to the thickness of the glass, in this case, a foil of 5mm for a 3 mm piece of glass. Fix it by starting to stick it on one of the sides, near to a corner, and in such a way that the edge stays in the centre of the foil.

2

2 Continue sticking the foil carefully along the edge whilst turning the piece, folding it over the edges.

3 Finish by sticking the finishing end on to the starting end of the foil and cutting it with shears. It is not advisable for the joining point of the two ends to be on an edge as this can cause problems with the soldering.

3

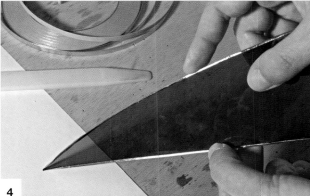

4

4 First fix the side of the foil onto the sides of the glass by pressing down with your fingers.

5 Next, smooth down the surfaces and the cut or outline with the lead knife. This process ensures the correct adhesion of the foil and removes any thickness, thus ensuring the pieces fit correctly.

5

Copper foil of different widths is used (in this case 4.8, 5.2 and 6 mm) depending on the thickness of each piece of glass. The application of foil on extremely curved edges should be done carefully otherwise it can break on the sides and open. If this happens re-cut the part with the breaks with a cutter.

Place the pieces of glass with the copper foil onto the drawing and check that they fit then join them with masking tape.

Assembly

Once the edging is completed, to continue on to the assembly all the pieces have to be placed on the scale drawing (see page 34) on the assembly table. After checking that they correspond to the design and fit together, stick masking tape on to the joints. To fix it together on the table strips can be nailed to the work surface as a frame to work on the whole piece and then the pieces are laid out inside or a fixing system similar to that of leading can be used. For this, fix the outside of the piece with nails or tacks onto the assembly table, these should be nailed leaning slightly outwards with a piece of lead in between to protect the glass. When the nail is touching the copper foil there is no need to protect it.

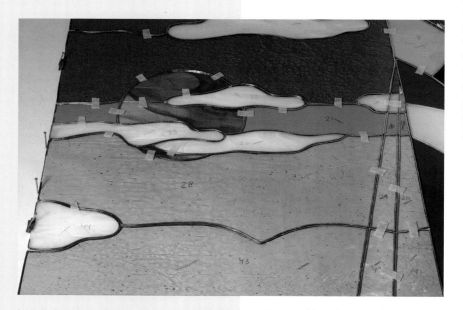

Join all the pieces of glass and fix the outside pieces to the assembly table with nails to avoid any movement or displacement.

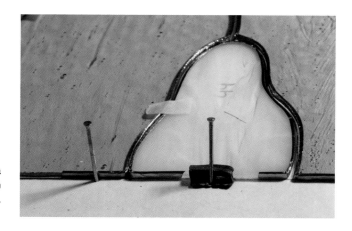

Protect the pieces of glass by inserting a fragment of lead strip. In the areas with copper foil no protection is needed.

Soldering

The soldering of work in copper foil is carried out in successive phases. First apply flux for copper under the foil on the joints of the pieces and solder (using a solder alloy of 60% solder and 40% lead) bringing the rod and the soldering iron to the point and depositing a drop of solder onto it. Once the joining points are done remove the masking tape and continue with the final soldering which is done in two stages. Firstly, apply flux onto the foil and solder by applying melted solder with the soldering iron onto the whole surface of the joint; next go over this with the soldering iron to join up the surface of the solder, thus making the joint line as even as possible. Work on one surface first and then the other. The creative use of soldering with solder is a significant visual area for making pieces, and constitutes another method for this technique (this can be seen step by step on pages 98-107).

FLAT PIECES

Soldering flat pieces is done by following the steps described. Once the joints are done the soldering is done with a continuous movement, gradually moving the soldering iron and the rod at the same time so that the solder penetrates and an even surface is achieved. Then this is gone over a second time with the soldering iron to obtain an even border.

1

2

1 Apply flux for copper onto the joints of the pieces making sure its does not touch the skin. It is advisable to work in a well ventilated area.

2 Put the bar of solder onto the point and bring the soldering iron for copper close. The solder will liquefy quickly and will stay on the head of the soldering iron, with which it is applied to the copper.

3 First, all of the connecting parts are soldered together at the junctions.

3

Basic techniques

4 Remove the masking tape and apply flux on the whole area of copper foil to be worked.

4

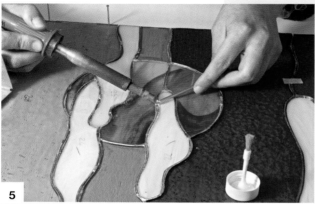

5

6

5 Apply the first phase of the solder, moving the rod and soldering iron over the copper foil at the same time. The solder penetrates between the pieces and results in strong solder.

6 Go over the areas a second time with the tip of the soldering iron to even out the thickness and the appearance of the border. If necessary, solder can be added to any areas which need it.

7 The solder should have the appearance of a continuous border with a rounded surface which is as even as possible.

7

SHAPED PIECES

Soldering shaped pieces does not differ greatly from soldering flat pieces, although it requires a rather more complex process. The soldering of simple pieces, such as boxes or other containers is done by first making joining points on each side, pressing them together by hand. They are done one by one, until all the pieces are complete, resulting in a free standing piece. Next, each side is soldered one at a time as explained previously. The creation of more complex pieces, such as lampshades, require the use of a mold as support (see pages 108-115)

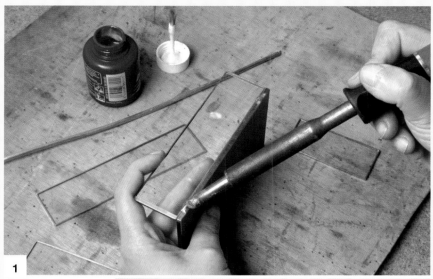

1

1 To make boxes or other simple containers first solder one of the sides to the base with two joining points.

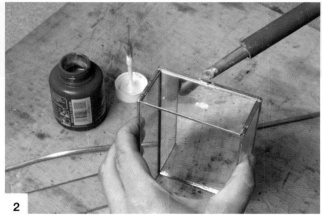

2

2 The work is done piece by piece, first the larger sides are fixed and then the smaller ones, by putting a drop of solder on the base and another on each side.

3 Once all the sides are joined they are soldered by following the process described previously, and making the border of each side one by one

3

Basic techniques

Cleaning

The final process in the copper foil technique consists of a total clean of the work to remove the leftover flux from the glass and the dirt produced during the assembly and soldering; equally it prepares the pieces for the later application of patina if desired. Wash all the surfaces with water and detergent and, next, dry them completely with a clean cotton cloth. If you want the solder joints to appear shiny then rub them hard with the cloth. To clean large areas use sponges, scourers or cloths, and to remove the leftover flux in the nooks and crannies and hard to reach places use a synthetic hair brush, for example, a tooth brush.

To remove the flux and dirt on the work, wash it with a sponge soaked in soapy water.

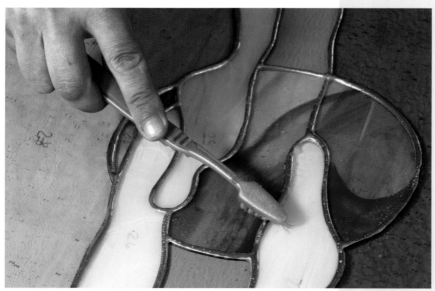

To remove the pieces of dirt incrusted in the edges and nooks and crannies use a synthetic tooth brush.

Patinas

Once the cleaning process is complete, the joints show the color of the solder and are shiny. In some cases, it will be necessary to apply a patina to vary the color of the joints to blend with the color scheme of the work. With this they can be made to appear dark or opaque due to oxidization and will not contrast too much with the glass, becoming part of the whole color scheme. It is not advisable to use patina on the solder lines of joints with glass previously worked on with a painting material such as grisaille, enamel or silver stain, as they can attack the decoration which has already been fired. After applying a patina leave it to work for a period which depends on the product and the instructions of the manufacturer. Next, it is removed by rubbing with a clean cloth, which can be slightly dampened, in order to completely remove the product. In this case protective gloves must be used.

1 Once any traces of flux have been cleaned off the patina is applied with a paintbrush. A sponge or a cloth can also be used in which case protective gloves must be used. In this example it is a copper sulphate which gives a blackish effect.

2 Leave the patina to work for the time recommended by the manufacturer which, in some cases, can be 12 hours, depending on the desired shade, others work in less time.

3 Lastly, remove the patina by rubbing with a clean cloth.

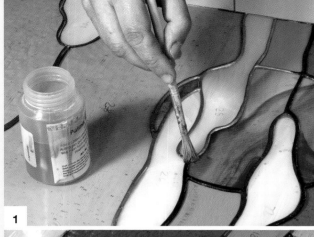

1

2

3

Clean soldering appears bright and the color of the solder vividly stands out from the colors of the glass. Once the patina has been applied the lines of solder integrate completely with the object.

Step
by step

This section shows in detail a series of step by step exercises which cover the complete leaded glass process, from the initial planning to the finished piece. It is made up of six exercises which suggest ideas for the creative process and in which the possibilities of this artistic field are explained, including glasswork. They show objects made with copper foil techniques and others with a combination of the two techniques, that is, leading and copper foil.

Making
a **mobile**

This exercise explains the process of making a mobile, a moving sculpture with pieces in the shape of leaves, entitled Fall, originally by Julia Rodríguez. It shows one of the possibilities offered by copper foil other than that of its use for joints with solder, as it is used to finish off the outside of the pieces of glass and to fix the supports of the pieces. In this case, the glass is worked first directly with grisaille, enamel, and silver stain.

1

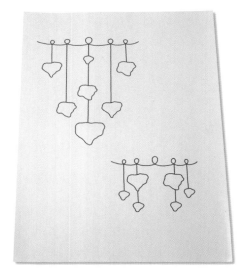

2

1 The design of the mobile is drawn in color on paper, showing the pieces and the holding system of the whole pieces, from two twisted rods.

2 The parts making up the piece are planned from the original design. The upper part is composed of a bar with six leaves and the lower part of another, longer, bar with seven leaves.

3 The templates for each shape are drawn on white paper and numbered to show how many pieces of glass must be cut of each one. In this case, there are one piece of 9.3 x 10.5 cm for the largest leaf, three pieces of 6.5 x 7.8 cm for the medium-sized leaves, four pieces of 6.9 x 7.7 cm for the smaller leaves and five pieces of 5.2 x 5.5 cm for the smallest leaves.

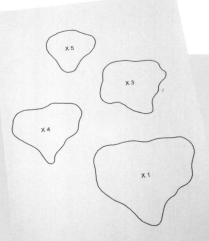

3

4 Next, the shapes are placed onto kraft paper and cut with ordinary scissors to create the templates for cutting.

5 Using the templates as a guide cut all the shapes in glass. Two types of textured class are used, 3 and 2.5 mm thick, respectively. Cut the pieces in both types of glass with the same shape so they can later be combined when the mobile is assembled.

6 Clean the pieces of glass and outline the edge of each of them with grisaille, marking the shape of the leaves and of the central veins, and leave them to dry. Place the pieces in a kiln for a firing cycle with a slow rise in temperature, from room temperature to 600 °C in 20 minutes. Turn the kiln off and let the pieces cool down inside until they return to room temperature.

Step by step

7

8

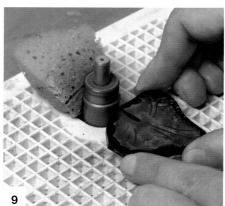

9

7 Now, green enamel can be applied to the central part of the leaves. Leave to dry and carry out a firing cycle similar to the previous one.

8 Lastly, apply silver stain to the outer parts of the leaves. Leave to dry and carry out a firing cycle similar to the previous ones.

9 Polish the edges of all the pieces with the side polisher to ensure that the copper foil will stick easily.

10 Dry the pieces and remove any residue left on the glass with a clean cloth. Edge the pieces: for this, stick the foil, perfectly centered, on the edges of the pieces of glass and fix the finishing end a little over the starting end. For the 2.5 mm thick pieces of glass use 4.8 mm wide foil and for the 3 mm thick pieces, 5.2 mm wide foil.

10

"Polish the edges of all the pieces with the side polisher to ensure that the copper foil will stick easily."

11 To stick the foil well press down with your finger, then smooth the surfaces and the edge with the lead knife to ensure the correct adhesion and to remove any thicker parts.

12 Apply the flux onto the area of copper foil which covers one of the faces of the pieces.

13 Next, cover the whole area of the foil with solder, moving the rod and the soldering iron at the same time. Once the soldering of one side is complete, continue the process on the other side.

14 Apply flux to the sides of the pieces and also cover them with solder. Move the tip of the soldering iron in an even fashion to obtain a continuous surface.
Repeat this with all the pieces.

15

15 To make the supports for the mobile use a metal rod 3.5 mm in diameter, in order to hold the metal rings 5 mm in diameter, and nylon thread and crimp beads to fix the ends of the threads. To protect the surface of the rod use a varnish especially for metals.

16 Make the supports for the leaves by placing a ring on the central part of the upper edge of each leaf like a stalk (in some cases two, as in the original design). Hold the ring perfectly straight with pincers, apply flux and fix with a layer of solder placing a drop of solder on the joint with the soldering iron. Repeat with the other leaves which are then washed and dried.

16

"*Apply a patina of copper sulphate onto the coat of solder, ensuring that it does not touch the glass.*"

17 With a paintbrush, apply a patina of copper sulphate onto the coat of solder, ensuring that it does not touch the glass. Leave to dry for a few minutes and rub with a clean cloth.　　17

18 To make the two supports of the mobile cut two rods, one approximately 50 cm and the other 40 cm in length. Bend them at regular intervals like the original design twisting it around a rod of iron fixed in a vise.

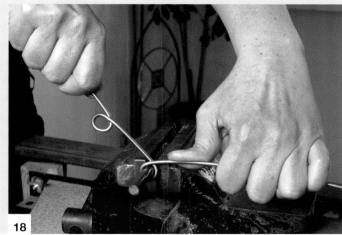

18

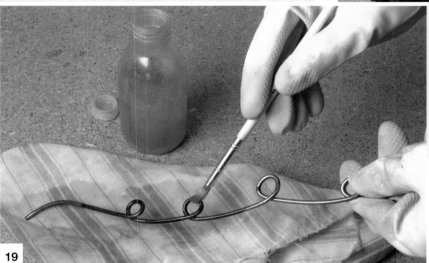

19

19 Apply patina of copper sulphate with a paintbrush and leave for around twelve hours. Next, clean with a cloth.

20 Then apply a coat of protective varnish especially for metals and leave to dry. Next straighten the end of the rods pushing them upwards.

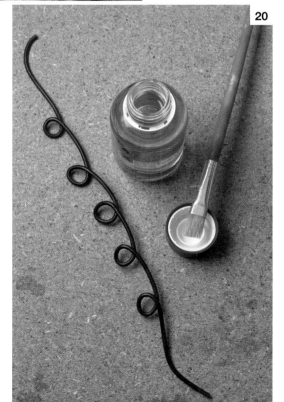

20

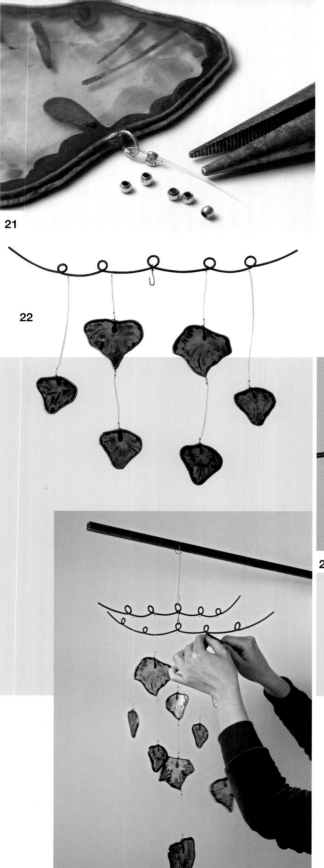

21 Now pass the nylon thread inside the rings and fix them with the help of a crimp bead. This is placed in the desired position, close to the end of the thread on the upper part of the ring, and squeeze with the pincers to fix it.

22 Repeat the process assembling the leaves on the shorter support (which will appear in the upper part) with the same system. Also fix the two lower leaves which hang from the central ones. The length of the threads will be similar for each pair of leaves.

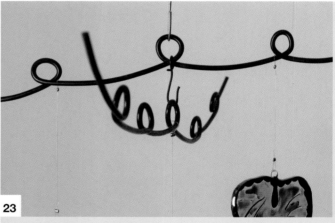

23 To work more easily, hang the upper support on a hook and place the lower part of the mobile on it, joining the first with a piece of curved wire like the hook which has already had patina applied.

24 Next, fix the leaves by following the system described with the help of the crimp beads. Take great care to ensure that the whole piece is perfectly level.

The finished mobile

Light
sculpture

This section, showing the work of Maria Puig shows the process of creating a light sculpture made with opaline Favrile glass with the copper foil technique. The visual characteristics of the glass, which show washes of reddish color mixed with others of opaline white, become the main feature of this work. To make it, the cutting is planned in such a fashion that the sides of the finished sculpture appear with continuous shapes even with the displacement of the sides.

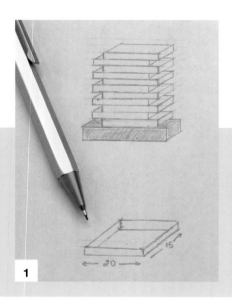

1 Make the sketch for the drawing, the shapes are based on the repetition by height of pieces made of sheets of glass of 20 and 15 cm long and 2.5 cm wide, which will be moved from bottom to top.

2 To visualize the effect of the work, a model is made to scale with cardboard. This will help to set out the cutting of the glass and as a guide during the whole process.

2

3

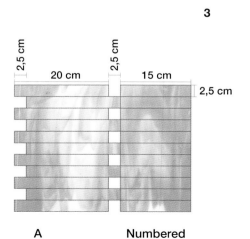

A   Numbered

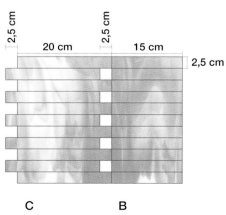

C   B

3 Take two sheets of the same type of glass and mark the cutting lines as they appear on the diagram. On one of the sheets mark the pieces of two of the sides and on the other mark the pieces of the other two sides, in such a way that those of 15 cm in length always appear aligned whilst those of 20 cm are displaced alternatively, with those of side A complementing those of side C.

4 Cut the pieces of sides C and B perfectly straight with the cutter and the help of the set square. With the cutter mark lines where the pieces at the ends which will be discarded (in white in the diagram)

5 and **6** Next, cut the sides of A and those of the numbered side, as well as the pieces at the ends to be discarded. The cut pieces fit the cutting diagram perfectly.

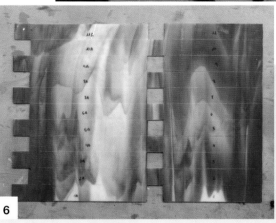

7 Polish the edges of all the pieces to ensure the copper foils sticks properly, then clean them with a cloth.

8 Now edge all of the pieces with copper foil 5.2 mm wide, as the pieces of glass are 3 mm thick. For this, stick the foil on the edge of the pieces of glass, centering them perfectly and fix the end of the foil a little over the top. Press down with your fingers and then with the lead knife to ensure it is fixed properly.

8

9

9 With a paintbrush apply flux on the upper and lower surfaces of the pieces of glass on top of the copper foil.

10

10 Solder the surface of the copper foil by moving the rod and the soldering iron at the same time to achieve an even surface.

11 Continue in the same fashion on the smaller size of each piece covering the copper foil with solder.

11

12 12 To carry out the assembly nail two square rods of 1cm thick (21.5 x 25 cm long) in a right angle on to the wooden top of the assembly table.

13

13 13 Next, lean the piece of side A onto the horizontal rod and the piece of the numbered side onto the vertical rod, in such a way that the vertices converge. Apply flux and solder the join.

14 14 Turn the piece around and lean side A onto the vertical rod, and the piece of side B onto the horizontal rod. Next, apply flux and solder as in the previous step.

15 15 After soldering the join of the piece of side C leaning it on the horizontal rod with side B and the numbered side.

14

"Solder by moving the rod and the soldering iron at the same time to achieve an even surface."

15

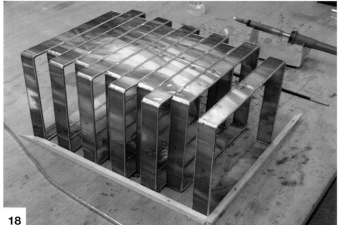

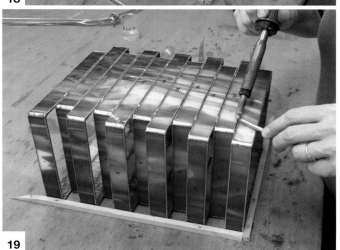

16 Apply flux and solder the four joining vertices of the sides of each of the eleven layers of the sculpture.

17 The underneath of each layer is also soldered.

18 To join the different parts or layers also use the wooden rods used as a guide. Place the piece with one of the bigger sides onto the table using the rods as a buffer and, next, place the following piece in the same way (with the sides that correspond A-A, B-B, C-C and number with number), but moved 2.5 cm as in the model.

19 Fix the whole piece with part A towards you, and apply flux to a couple of points and solder.

20

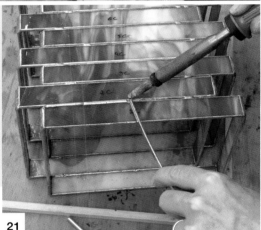

21

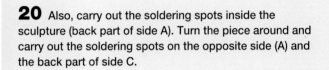
20 Also, carry out the soldering spots inside the sculpture (back part of side A). Turn the piece around and carry out the soldering spots on the opposite side (A) and the back part of side C.

21 Apply flux to the outside joins and solder by moving the rod of solder and the soldering iron evenly to achieve a continuous soldered surface.

"The pieces are soldered so that the sides correspond (A-A, B-B, C-C and number with number)"

22

23

22 Then, solder the joins of the inside of the sides of the sculpture.

23 Once all the soldering is complete, clean the sculpture with water and detergent to remove any remains of solder and dry with a clean cloth.

24 With a cloth apply a patina of copper sulphate to the solder. Leave it to work for a few minutes and polish with a clean cloth.

24

25

25 Ask a metalworker to make a sheet metal base measuring 27.7 x 20.7 cm for the base and with a height of 5.2 cm. Request a central hole to place the bulbholder for the lamp and for four L-shaped 1 cm pieces to fix the sculpture.

26 Place the piece on the base, center it with respect to the sides, and place the L-shaped pieces. Then, fix these with screws; note that they do not appear centered on the base. Paint the whole base with wrought iron type metallic finish enamel and install the electrical components.

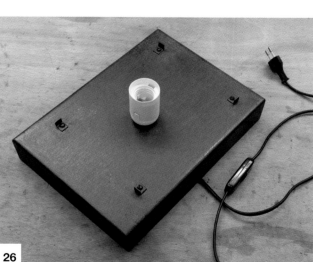

26

The light sculpture mounted on the base and lit from inside.

Box with
creative **soldering**

This example explains the making of a box using the copper foil method, with a mirrored base and a lid made of different types of glass by Julia Rodríguez. Here, the lid is the focus of attention, and it is a piece with great creativity. It shows off the use of creative soldering by making soldered dots as a method for highlighting the visual rhythms of the joints, which constitute a fundamental element of this composition.

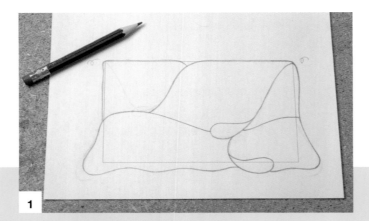

1 A box will be made with a container measuring 3.5 x 8 x 14 cm. For this, first the lid is designed, which will overhang the container slightly. Draw the shape of the pieces and the placement of the rings which will hold it.

2 From the design choose the pieces of glass, in this case different types of textured glass. The light blue, mid blue and yellow pieces of glass are of a smooth color and the orange glass and the glass with blue washes are Favrile glass.

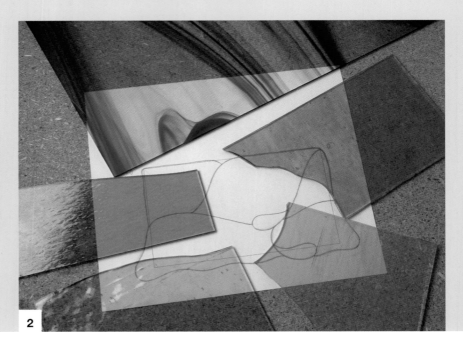

3 Cut a 8 x 14 cm piece of mirror, 3mm thick, with the help of a set square.

3

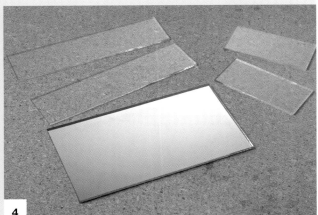

4

4 Also, cut two pieces of 3.5 x 14 cm and two of 3.5 x 7.5 cm of colorless glass, 2 mm thick.

5 Polish all the sides of the pieces to ensure the correct adhesion of the copper foil and clean them.

6 Edge the smaller pieces of colorless glass and one of the larger pieces with copper foil 3.9 mm wide. This foil is stuck on and centered, and fixed to the end by slightly overlaying the beginning of the strip, pressed down with fingers and then with the lead knife.

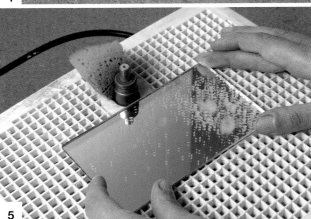

5

6

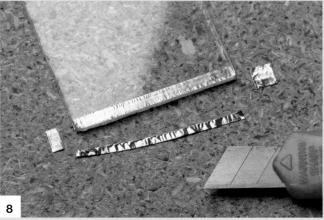

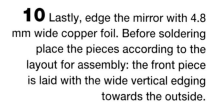

7 Edge the two vertical sides of the same face of the 14 cm piece (which will configure the front of the box) with copper foil 4.8 mm wide, situated 2 mm onto the face of the glass.

8 Cut the remaining foil with the cutter.

9 In this way, the foil of the front pieces covers the join with the side pieces and gives a clean appearance. Next, edge the piece with the 3.9 mm wide copper foil.

10 Lastly, edge the mirror with 4.8 mm wide copper foil. Before soldering place the pieces according to the layout for assembly: the front piece is laid with the wide vertical edging towards the outside.

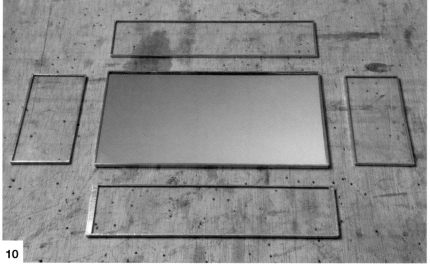

11

12

13 Continue in the same way with the piece of the back side and then with the side pieces, which are placed on the base and the inside part of the larger sides.

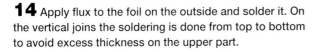

14 Apply flux to the foil on the outside and solder it. On the vertical joins the soldering is done from top to bottom to avoid excess thickness on the upper part.

15 Flux is also applied to the upper edges of the container and then soldered.

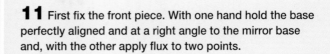

11 First fix the front piece. With one hand hold the base perfectly aligned and at a right angle to the mirror base and, with the other apply flux to two points.

12 Move the tip of the soldering iron to the rod placed on the work table, take a small amount of solder and solder the points.

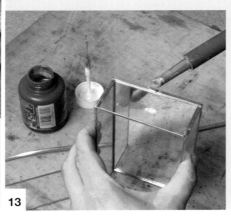

13

"Before soldering place the pieces according to the layout for assembly"

14

15

16 Cut four pieces of about 0.8 cm of silver colored metal wire of 0.8 mm in diameter and bend them in the shape of a bobby pin with pliers.

16

17 Then solder the pins into the upper vertex of the back corner of the container. Hold them with the help of some pincers, apply flux to the join and solder.

18 Clean the container with water and detergent to remove the flux and then dry it.

17

18

"To shape forms with very pronounced waves use the polisher"

19 Now draw the design of the lid onto kraft paper by tracing it with tracing paper. Cut the cutting templates with glass pattern shears for copper.

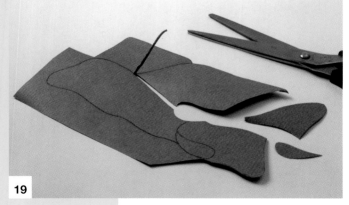

19

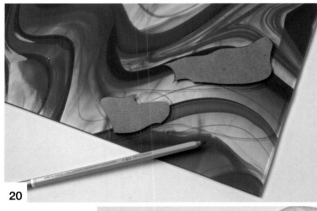

20 The templates are placed in the desired layout on the sheet of glass (in this case, on a blue wave), turned downwards on the back of the pieces of glass, as they have less relief. Mark the shape with wax pencil leaving some space and cut the pieces.

20

21 Cut the shape of each piece with the help of the templates. To shape forms with very pronounced waves use the polisher. Then polish the edges of all the pieces and clean the glass.

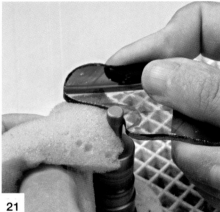

21

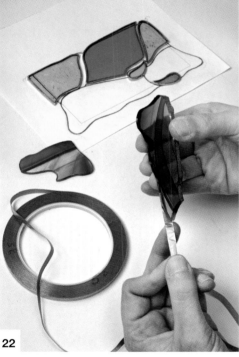

22 Edge all the pieces. For those made with blue Favrile glass use copper foil 5.6 mm wide. Place it perfectly in the center and fix the end by overlaying the beginning end, pressing down first with fingers and then with the lead knife.

22

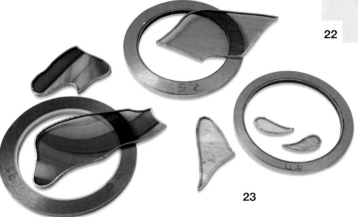

23 For the remaining pieces use foil of 4.8 mm and of 5.2 mm, according to the thickness.

23

Step by step

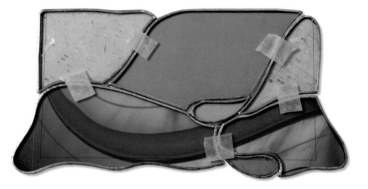

24

*"Make decorative dots
with the solder"*

24 Place the pieces onto the assembly template and fix then with masking tape.

25 After apply flux and solder the joining points, then remove the masking tape.

26 Also apply flux onto the join lines and solder by applying solder with the soldering iron.

27 Continue soldering each piece in order. If necessary, go over the soldering again with the soldering iron to even up the surface.

25

26

27

28 At the end of some soldering and on the central part of the upper right soldering make some decorative dots with the solder.

29 Once the upper side is complete, solder the bottom side.

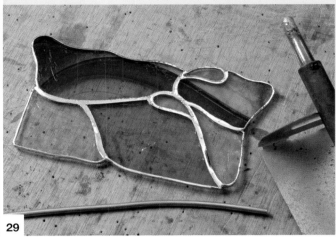

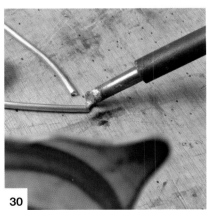

30 Lastly, solder the outside edges and the inside of the lid. With the tip of the soldering iron collect a small amount of solder from the rod on the work table.

31 Next, place it on the foil moving the soldering iron. Clean with water and detergent and dry.

32 To fix the lid to the container pass a pin through the ring, place the lid in the right position, apply flux and solder. Afterwards, clean it.

32

33 To protect the mirror from any scratches which will spoil it, stick a sheet of black sticky back plastic with a velvet side to it.

33

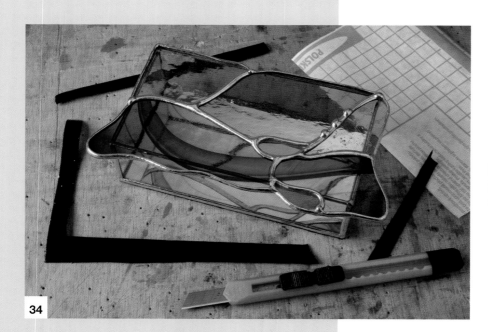

34

34 Cut the leftover parts off with a cutter.

The finished box.

Lampshade

This exercise shows the creation of a large lampshade, designed for a floor lamp, made with the copper foil technique. The piece, designed by Maria Puig, is loosely based on the visual repertoire of Catalan modernism. The difficulty of this exercise lies in the fact that it is a piece with volume where the pieces are assembled onto a three dimensional mold. Note that the sharper the curvature of the lampshade the smaller the pieces are.

1 Various 40 x 26 Porexpan molds for lampshades of the same shape have been acquired and the original design has been designed to go over one of them. The shade will be made up of five equal parts.

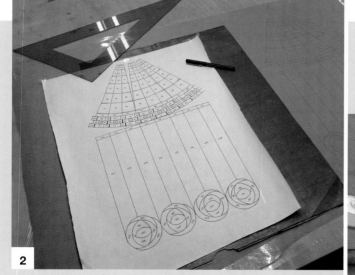

2 Draw the shapes onto a flat template, number all of them and trace them onto card with tracing paper. Next, cut them to make the cutting templates.

3 Using the cutting templates as models cut the pieces of glass. Afterwards, number them with a permanent marker pen.

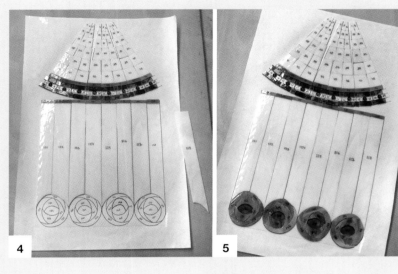

4 and **5** The upper and central parts of the lampshade are made with white opaque glass, whilst the central curved areas and the lower border are made of different types of glass: Favrile, flashed, colorless, iridescent and molded. Cut all the pieces and place them on the assembly templates, working in parallel on the five parts making up the lampshade.

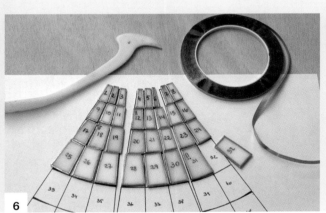

6 Polish all the pieces, clean them and edge them with copper foil.

7 and **8** Work in order, placing the pieces once they are edged onto the templates until the five parts are finished.

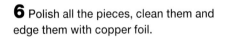

8

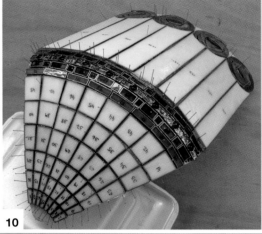

9

10

9 The assembly and soldering are carried out on the model. To avoid the solder melting the Porexpan apply a coat of silicon onto the mold and leave to dry. Assemble the pieces on the model.

10 Fix them in the marked layout on the model, holding the lower and side parts with pins nailed to the Porexpan.

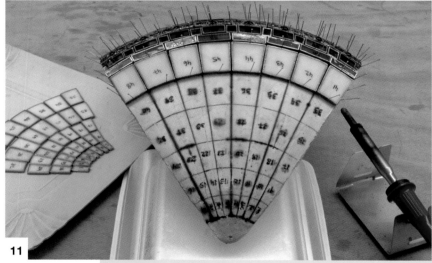

11

12

11 First solder the upper part of the lampshade, remove part of the pieces and lay them out in order on to a tray or another transportable surface.

12 Solder the pieces nearest to the curves; for this, apply flux to the points where the white pieces intersect with the Favrile glass pieces.

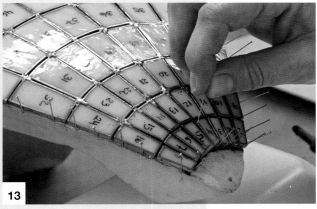

13

14

13 Next, place the next row of pieces at the bottom, securing them with pins and soldering the joins. Continue in this fashion until the lowest row. The small pieces can be fit with a pin to ensure the correct placement.

14 Finish the soldering of the joints of the upper part of the lampshade.

15 Now, solder the points of the curved area; apply flux and solder the joints of the pieces.

16 Lastly, solder the points of the pieces that make up the lower shapes of the lampshade.

15

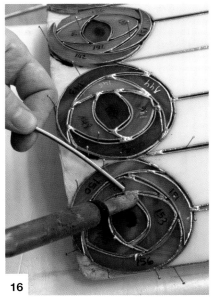

16

"The assembly and soldering are carried out on the model, with the pieces held in place with pins."

17

18

17 Carefully remove the piece from the mold and then, continue in the same fashion with the other four parts which make up the lampshade. Note the appearance of one of the parts with soldering on the points.

18 Once the five pieces are complete place them on a support (in this case plastic packaging) to avoid any breaks or faults. Assemble by joining two of the parts, using the models as support and soldering the joints.

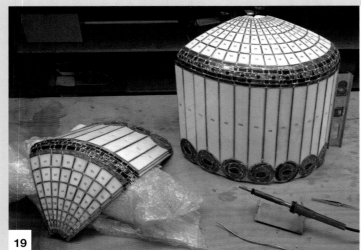

19

19 The assembly must be carried out on a straight surface by using a reliable system of support; it is necessary to check that the sides are perfectly level.

20 Continue assembling and soldering the remaining parts with the help of the models, and keep checking the sides are vertical. To avoid displacements tie the whole piece with a band.

20

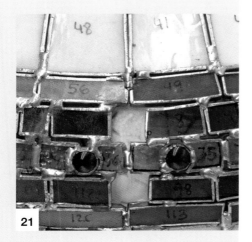

21 When planning the joints of the parts making up the lampshade spaces without pieces were left, now allowing for perfect adjustment of the joints.

22 Make the pink pieces which are missing (cut, polish and edge) and join them by soldering.

"The assembly must be carried out checking that it is level and the pieces fit perfectly"

23 Now put the whole piece inside a large flowerpot, packed with straw to avoid any movement, and solder the inside. Apply flux and solder all the joints and the edge.

24 Carefully remove the lampshade and place it vertically on a low soft, but firm work surface. Apply flux and solder the joints of the upper part.

Step by step

25 Turn the lampshade around and lay it on its side. To avoid any displacement put a piece of sponge inside, which will hold the piece together and fix the models being used as a base.

26 Next, apply flux to the join lines and solder them. Always work on the area with the support models inside; when the soldering is complete change their position and continue the work.

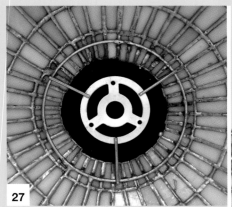

27 Place the support right in the centre of the lampshade (which will fix the shade to the stand) and join by applying flux and soldering.

28 Also, fix the support or outer bulbholder right in the centre, applying flux and then soldering.

29 Apply flux to the whole surface of the bulbholder. Apply a coat of solder which is spread with the soldering iron.

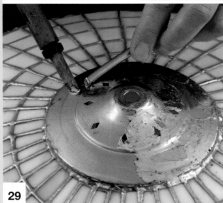

The lampshade once the patina is applied and it is completely clean, assembled on a bronze stand with patina.

Making a wall light
with different techniques

The next section shows how to create a wall light made with leading and copper foil technique. The work is done in two phases. In the first the front part is made with the copper foil technique using molded glass and also different pieces of glass previously worked on with enamel, silver stain and sandblasting. In the second, the front support and the lower part of the lamp are made by the leading technique. Piece by Julia Rodríguez.

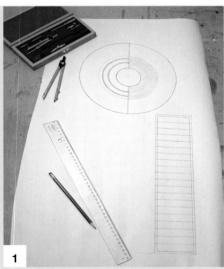

1 To start, make the plan for the shapes of the wall light. It will consist of a front circular part of 25 cm in diameter in total composed of two pieces of glass, a central disc of 6.3 cm in diameter and a lower part of 9 x 39 cm which will be placed around it composed of 20 pieces of glass.

2 Trace the shape of the front pieces on to kraft paper to make the cutting template.

3 Then cut the templates and use them as a guide for cutting the two pieces, one of colorless antique glass and the other of blue textured glass around 3.5 mm thick. Check that the disc fits and clean the pieces of glass.

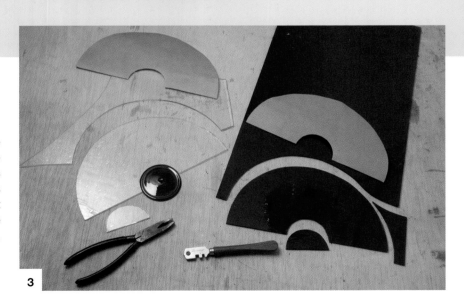

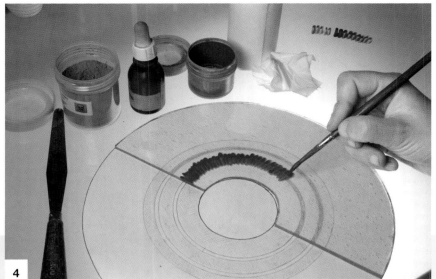

4 Now place the colorless glass with the design template onto a light table. Using this as a guide, apply blue enamel onto the marked area (3 mm wide and separated 1.9 cm from the center) with crossing brushstrokes. Leave it to dry.

5 Continue in this fashion with the silver stain on an area similar to the previous one, separated from it by 1.1 cm and 0.9 from the outer circumference. Leave it to dry.

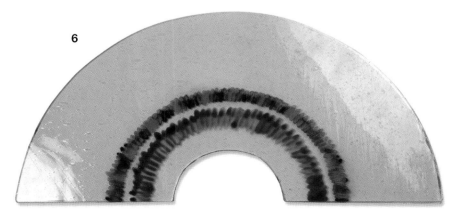

6 After drying, carry out a firing cycle with a slow rise from room temperature to 600 °C in 20 minutes, after which turn the kiln off and leave the glass to cool down inside.

7 Now make the shields. Place the glass onto the template on the work table and stick a sheet of sticky back plastic to its surface. With a sharp knife cut around the lines marked on the template.

8 Remove the parts of the sheet which cover the central part, the part between the two colors, and between the silver stain and the outside line.

9 With the other piece continue in the same fashion. Make the cuts on the sheet from the marks on the design and remove the central parts, the parts between the lines and the outer part.

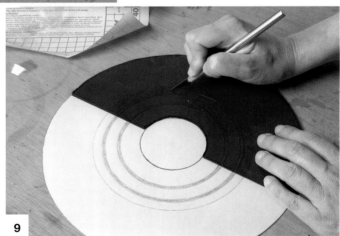

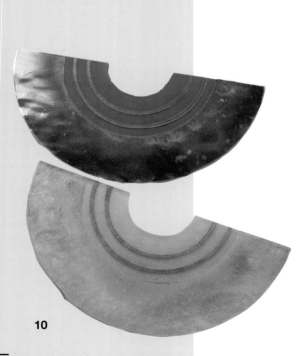

10 Work on the two pieces by sandblasting them. Remove the shields and clean the glass with water and detergent.

11   12

*"The parts covered with shields stay shiny, whilst
the rest appears matte."*

13

14

11 The parts covered with shields
stay shiny, whilst the rest appears
matt. Polish the inside edges of
both pieces.

12 Also polish the lower part of the
edge and the outer border of the disc.
Clean all the pieces.

13 Edge the disc with copper foil
4.88 mm wide. Also edge the inner
edge and outer part, (see picture) of
the pieces worked on with
copper foil 5.6 mm.

14 Now assemble the piece, apply
flux to the joins and solder.

15

"Apply flux to all the joins and solder by applying solder with the soldering iron."

15 Apply flux to all the joins and solder by applying solder with the soldering iron to the surface of the join.

16 Next turn the piece around and put it on a soft support (in this case, plastic packaging) to avoid any breakage. Then, solder the back part.

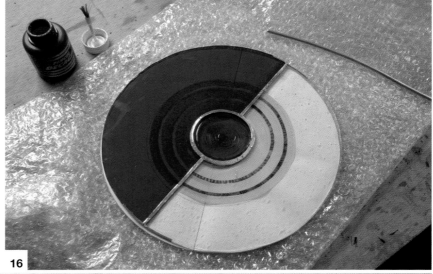

16

17 In this step the outside of the piece is leaded. For this, put it on the assembly table and hold it on one of its sides with tacks, inserting a fragment of lead.

17

18

19

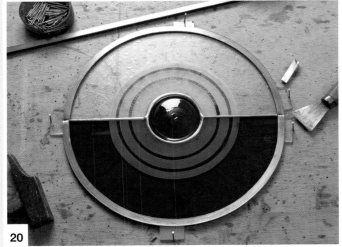

20

18 Put contact adhesive on the heart, inside the 8 mm lead came.

19 Then lead the upper part of the wall light by inserting the colorless glass inside the strip. Fix with tacks, inserting fragments of glass, and cut the end with the cutter right on the previous soldering.

20 Remove the tacks holding the lower part and next lead the blue glass following the previous method.

21

21 Continuing with the same process fit a second lead by putting the lower wing of the second lead came into the heart of the first and the upper wing on top of it.

22 Flatten the wings of the front lead cames with the lead knife, pressing down at the same time as moving it along the surface.

23 To join the lead cames extend the line of existing solder sticking copper foil on the join of the edges.

24 Apply flux and solder to extend the line, as in the previous step.

25 After, remove the tacks holding the piece, turn it and place it on plastic packaging to avoid any damage and flatten the leads with the lead knife. Apply flux for lead to the joints of the lead came and solder.

26

27

"To join the lead cames extend the line of existing solder sticking copper foil on the join of the edges."

26 Now start to make the side cutting 18 rectangular pieces 8 cm long and 1.9 cm wide and 2 pieces of 8 x 2.4 cm orange textured glass.

27 Cut a 5mm lead came to around 42 cm long and place it perfectly aligned on the mark of the template. Check that the pieces of glass remain aligned with the upper inside line, fix with tacks and a long piece of glass.

28 Then apply contact adhesive inside the strip. Cut 21 strips of lead around 11 cm long and also apply contact glue to the two sides of the heart.

28

29

29 Place one of the 2.4 cm thick pieces of glass on the end, inserting it into the lower lead, and fix with tacks. Insert a lead strip inside of the wings of the lower one and fit the glass with the help of the cutter.

Step by step

30

30 Continue the process placing the lead cames and inserting the 1.9 cm pieces of glass as in the template. Lastly, place the 2.4 cm piece of glass on the end and finish with the final lead came.

31 Remove the leftover lead with the cutter. Make the cut aligned with the inner line of the template, 0.5 cm from the outer line.

32 Cut another piece of lead to about 42 cm, apply glue and lead the upper part of the piece. Fix with tacks and a long piece of glass and leave to dry for 12 hours.

33 Lastly, flatten all the lead cames, rounding them with the cutter.

"Using the template for the front part as a guide carefully curve the piece with the soldered part towards the inside until it fits the shape."

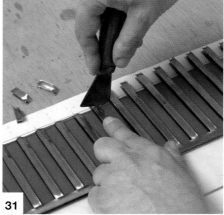

31

32

33

34

35

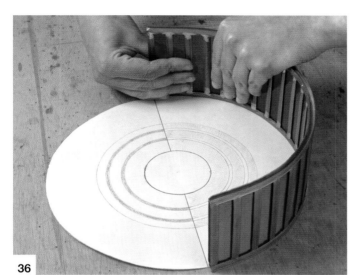

36

34 In this step, solder the inside of the piece. With a paintbrush, apply flux to the lead joints.

35 Next, solder the points. When this is finished, cut the leftover parts of the horizontal lead cames with a cutter and remove the tacks. Flatten the lead on the lower face.

36 Using the template for the front part as a guide carefully curve the piece with the soldered part towards the inside until it fits the shape.

37 With the lead knife lower the wings of the lead cames on the upper part.

37

Step by step

38 Then place the piece on the outside lead of the front piece, perfectly aligned with the inside part and fix it by soldering the two ends.

39 Also solder the outside at various points. Note that the back piece is a little removed from the leads at the front.

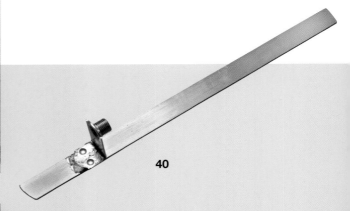

40 From a rod of brass 1.5 cm wide and 2 mm thick, cut a piece 25.3 cm long; cut the edges in a rounded fashion so they fit the wall light. Solder a 5.5 cm lamp support to one of the ends.

41 Solder the rod to the back part of the wall light, on top of the back perimeter leads. Lastly, install the electrical components and fix to the wall with hooks.

The wall light fixed onto a wall.

Mirror
with **light**

The following pages show the process for creating a mirror with light. The piece, made by Maria Puig, is made with the leading technique, using copper foil for the creation of some details where small pieces of glass are used. The steps explain how to make the mirror with different pieces of glass, the assembly and also the placement of a tailor made light box inside. The back light will emphasize the visual properties of each piece of glass.

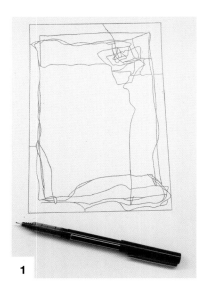

1 First of all, make the design of the piece, which will have a large central piece of mirror flanked by different types of glass.

2 Enlarge the original design by photocopying it to the total size of the piece, which will be 98.5 x 66.5 cm, to create an assembly template. Also make the cutting templates with kraft paper.

3 Then place a copy of the template onto the light table and choose the pieces of glass with which to create the piece. In this case, they will be pieces of glass of different types: flashed glass in orange, pink and two shades of brown, opalescent Favrile glass with yellow and pink washes of different types and iridescent colorless glass.

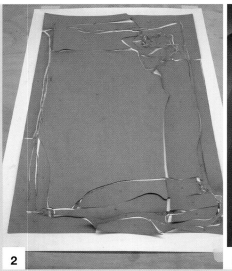

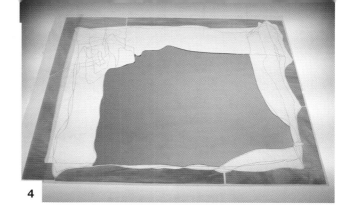

4

4 First make the main piece of the work. With the template as a guide cut the central piece of mirror and place it on the template. Next, from the template, cut the pieces of Favrile glass in yellow shades which make up the outside frame.

5 and **6** Continue cutting other pieces of mirror for the outside perimeter and those of yellow and pink Favrile glass which frame the central mirror. The details are made with the flashed and textured glass as well as the Favrile glass in other shades.

7 Next place the template onto the assembly table and fix with masking tape; next place the central mirrored piece. Looking at the template see that in the central upper left part there is a small piece that will require copper for the joint; for this protect the back mark of the mirror with a protective product.

5

6

7

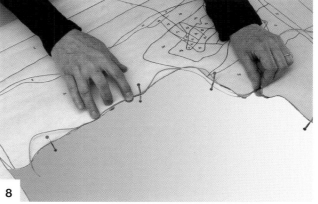

8

8 Place the mirror on the layout marked on the template and fix with glassmaker's tacks. Take the measurements for the lead for the upper part by going round the perimeter with a cord, which is more practical for wavy outlines.

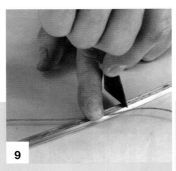

9 For this piece use 5 mm lead came. Transfer the measurement to a strip of lead and cut, leaving approximately 1 cm extra.

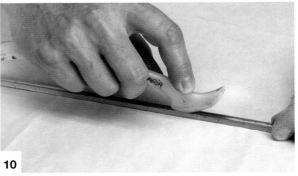

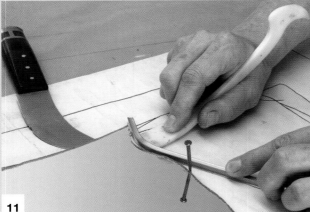

10 Then open the wings and straighten the strip by running curved part of the lead knife over the two sides of the heart.

11 Slightly raise the piece by inserting the tip of the curved cutting knife under it to facilitate the correct placement of the lead. Push the lead with the edge of the lead knife until the glass fits in perfectly.

12 Afterwards fix the lead with a tack, inserting a fragment of glass. Then continue along the rest of the upper part of the piece, fitting the lead to the wavy shapes of the glass.

13 Place the larger piece of Favrile glass along the perimeter of the mirror inside the lead. Here, it is slightly bigger than the shape marked on the template.

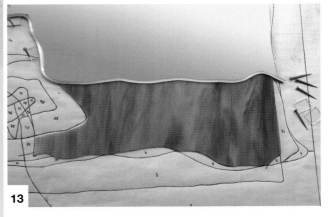

14

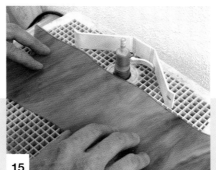

15

16

14 With a fine-tipped permanent marker mark the leftover part by following the curve of the lead.

15 and **16** Remove the excess part with the side polisher until the mark is reached. Then, fit the glass between the wings of the lead by lightly tapping with the handle of the hammer.

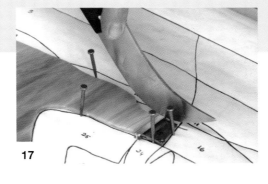

17

"The size of the pieces of glass can be adjusted removing the excess with the polisher"

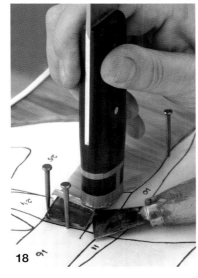

18

17 Next, fix the piece with glassmaker's tacks. Continue the work by leading the end and placing a piece of brown flashed glass. Cut the ends of the strip with a curved lead knife so that it fits the outline of the piece.

18 Flatten the ends. To do this, place the end of the cutter under the lead and tap with the handle of the curved lead knife.

Step by step

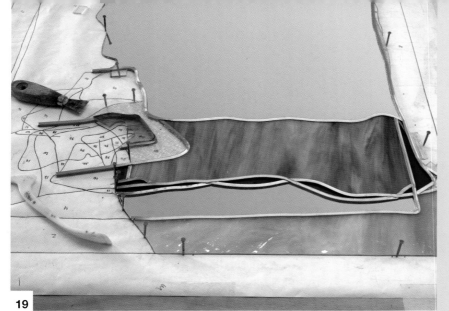

19

19 Continue with the assembly of the piece, by placing the pieces and leading them. When necessary, polish the pieces to ensure a correct fit.

20 For the joins of small pieces, use the copper foil technique after cleaning them. Put them on the template and continue leading other pieces.

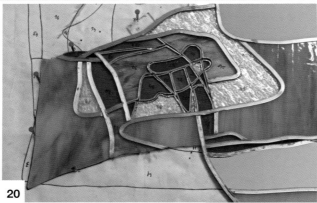

20

21 Once the upper part of the piece is complete, make the sides by placing the pieces and the lead cames according to the method described. Some joints have very tight corners; to solve this, first mark the cutting line with the permanent marker pen.

22 Cut along the mark with the cutter perfectly vertical.

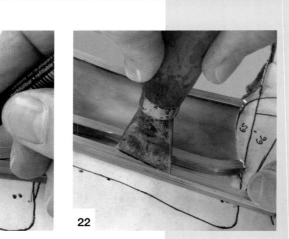

21

22

23 Then flatten the end to facilitate the correct fit into the side lead; this requires placing the end of the curved lead knife and tapping with a hammer.

23

24 Insert it between the wings of the side lead by pressing down with the lead knife or the cutter and fix it with a glass maker's tack and a piece of glass.

25 In this way it is possible to lead long pieces with very narrow ends.

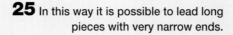

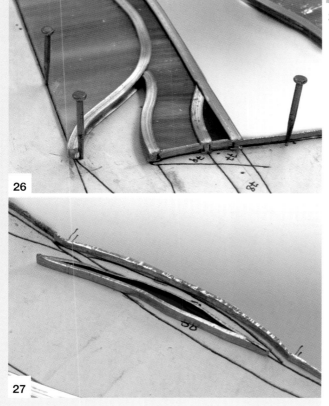

25

"The sides of the pieces of glass in contact with the copper covered pieces must be covered with copper foil"

26 Joining pieces of leaded glass with small pieces of glass with the copper foil technique requires the partial edging of the leaded pieces, covering the contact side with copper foil.

27 Cover the area of the mirror (previously treated with mirror protector) that will touch the copper covered piece with copper foil.

Step by step

133

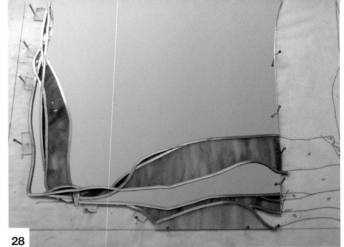

28 Place the side piece with copper foil and lead the other pieces of glass.

28

29

29 Then, continue placing the pieces laying out them out according to the template. Press the leads with the help of the cutters and place the copper covered pieces of glass.

30 Once one part is finished, place the outside pieces of Favrile glass in shades of yellow, in this case, on the upper part of the piece, and fix them with glass maker's tacks.

30

31 Work on them in order; first finish one part and then continue to finish another.

31

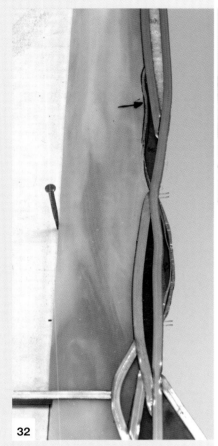

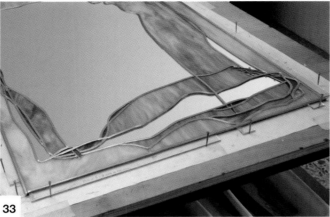

33

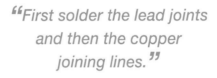

"First solder the lead joints and then the copper joining lines."

34

32

35

32 Now, assemble all the outside pieces. If there are any problems with fitting them mark the outline with a marker pen and remove the excess with the polisher.

33 The assembly is finished after the exterior leads of the piece, which in this case are 8 mm, are placed and the piece is held with glassmaker's tacks and some long fragments of glass.

34 Flatten the lead cames with the lead knife, then apply flux to the joints and solder.

35 Once the soldering of the lead cames is finished, apply flux to the copper joints and solder.

36 Remove the glassmaker's tacks and flatten the outside leads moving the curved lead knife to exert pressure.

36

Step by step

135

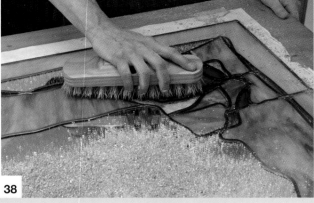

37 and **38** Apply putty with a palette knife, taking care that it penetrates all the gaps. Leave it to dry. Treat it with sawdust, pushing it into the corners with a bristle brush to remove all traces of the paste. Turn the piece over, flatten the leads on the back, and solder.

39 In a carpenter's workshop, framery, or another place that makes frames, ask for a box to be made with measurements of 115 x 83 x 11.5 cm in total, with an opening the size of the mirror and with a 1 cm slot to fit it. Assemble the electrical components, placing a fluorescent natural light tube on each side.

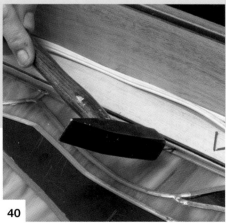

40 Disassemble the tubes and place the mirror inside, fitting it into the slot. First put it in vertically, then tip up one of the sides and place it completely horizontal. To adjust the fit and make sure it does not move, use some rods between the mirror and the frame, and nail with tacks. Finally, assemble the tubes again.

Appearance of the finished illuminated light.

Gallery

Julia Rodríguez. Vitraloi and Lourdes Perelló. *Dancing*, 2006. Painting made of glass with copper foil by Julia Rodríguez and hand painted silk by Lourdes Perelló (20 x 16 cm).

Julia Rodríguez. Vitraloi, *Spring*, 2007. Sculpture made of antique glass, Favrile glass, disc, copper foil, leading, wire and stone (50 x 25 cm).

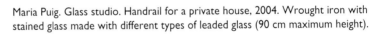

Maria Puig. Glass studio. Handrail for a private house, 2004. Wrought iron with stained glass made with different types of leaded glass (90 cm maximum height).

Marta Claverol. *Space dream*, 2006. Panel made with different types of glass worked on with grisaille, enamels, embossing, silkscreening and sandblasted and leaded (90 x 90 cm).

Julia Rodríguez. Vitraloi. Mobile, 2005. Mobile for an education and family leisure space in the Poble Espanyol in Barcelona. Made with different types of glass worked with enamels with copper foil, wire, shaped pieces, springs and bells among other elements (250 x 200 cm, approximately).

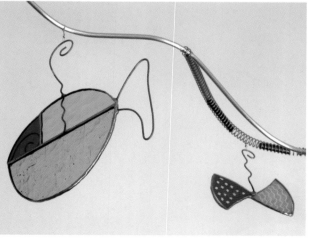

Details of the previous mobile where some of the elements and component pieces made with copper foil technique can be seen.

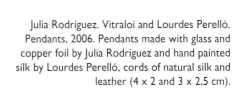

Julia Rodríguez. Vitraloi and Lourdes Perelló. Pendants, 2006. Pendants made with glass and copper foil by Julia Rodríguez and hand painted silk by Lourdes Perelló, cords of natural silk and leather (4 x 2 and 3 x 2,5 cm).

Julia Rodríguez. Vitraloi. *Teranyina*, 1999. Lamp made with textured glass with copper foil and wire (40 x 20 x 20 cm).

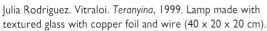

Julia Rodríguez. Vitraloi, *Lee*, 2005. Panel made with textured and antique glass, worked with fused enamel, copper foil and leading (40 x 30 cm).

B – **Barb.** Pieces of material that overhang unevenly from the edges or side of a piece of glass.

C – **Copper foil technique or covering with copper.** Technique of covering with copper foil. Copper foil is used as a base for soldering joints of the sides of the pieces of an object. This technique can be used for very small pieces, thin join lines, as well as making pieces with surface curves and is lighter than leading.
Cutter. Tool made of a handle with a cutting tip at one end and which is used for marking lines of weakness on glass.

E – **Enamel.** Mixture of metal oxides and finely ground glass powder that, mixed with water, forms a painting paste that is applied to the glass. By going through a firing cycle, the enamel (previously dry) fuses with the surface of the glass, giving it color.

F - **Firing cycle.** Cycle of heat which the glass goes through in the kiln. It is a heating phase from room temperature to the right temperature, depending on the piece and the later cooling phase
Fracture. Rupture of a mass when it goes over its limit of plasticity when force is applied.

G – **Grisaille.** Vitreous plaint composed of oxides and a binder. It comes in powder form and is prepared by mixing it with a vehicle to apply it onto glass. Once dry it goes through a firing cycle which fixes it to the surface of the glass.

L - **Lead came.** Strips of lead used to join pieces of glass with the leading technique. This material is toxic and requires the hands to be thoroughly washed afterwards.

Glossary

Lead cutting knife. Also called lead cutter. Tool composed of a steel blade and a handle used to cut lead to size.

Leading. Technique for assembling an object which consists in joining pieces of glass by inserting them sideways into the inside of strips or rods of lead (lead came), in contact with the heart and between the wings; then it is soldered, putty is applied and it is cleaned.

Lead knife. Also called an opener. Tool used for opening and straightening the lead came before assembling them.

Line of weakness. This is the line produced by the cutter on the glass and which marks where the cut is to be pressed on or tapped.

M – Matt. Translucent glass that has a matt surface. A matt surface can be achieved in the studio with a sandblasting machine.

P – Patina. Tone, color and quality that the surface of old objects have due to the passing of time; in addition, any substance that gives an aged appearance to a material.

S - Silver stain. Compound made of silver salts which, when mixed with water, form a painting paste that is applied to glass. Once dry and fired, it reacts chemically with the glass and colors it.

Solder. To join two pieces of metal solidly by fusing these pieces or by adding another metal.

T – Tiffany. Traditional name for the copper foil technique developed by Louis Comfort Tiffany at the end of the 19th century.

Bibliography

• Ainaud de Lasarte, A.; Mundó,
A. M.; Vila-Grau, J.; Escudero, A.;
Cañellas, S.; Vila, A.
*Els vitralls de la catedral de Barcelona
i del monestir de Pedralbes.* Institut
d'Estudis Catalans, Barcelona, 1997.

• Bubbico, G. y Crous, J. y G.
Tecniche e arte del vetro. Demetra,
Bolonia, 1999.

• Morr, A.
Contemporary Stained Glass. Mitchell
Beazley Publishers, London, 1989.

• Pizzoli, S. y D.
Manual práctico de la vidriería artística.
EDUNSA, Barcelona, 1993.

• Stephany, Erich y otros.
*Licht, Glas, Farbe: Arbeiten in Glas und
Stein aus den Rheinischen Werkstätten
Dr. Heinrich Oidtmann.* M. Brimberg,
Aquisgrán, 1982.

• Valldepérez, P.
El vitral. Parramón Ediciones,
Barcelona, 2004.

• Vila-Grau, J. y Rodón, F.
Las vidrieras modernistas catalanas.
Polígrafa, Barcelona, 1983.

Acknowledgements

The authors wish to thank
Parramón Ediciones, especially
María Fernanda Canal and Tomàs
Ubach for believing in us. Also,
thanks to Joan Soto and all the
team at Nos & Soto for their great
presentation. To Mònica Guilera,
who was fundamental in getting
this project underway and without
whom it would not have become
a reality, and also to Caterina
Hernández.

To Ángel Cuevas for his work
and unconditional support, to
Cosme Hierro and Joan Soler for
their help, to Ángel Requena and
Betty Pozo for their kindness in
letting us use their house to take
photographs and also to Roser
Giraben and Isidor Garriga for their
collaboration.

To my teacher
Antoni Gómez i Solagran,
who started me on leaded glass
and awakened a love in me
for this discipline
with his teaching.
Maria Puig

To the institutions
which have kindly collaborated:

El Poble Espanyol de Barcelona
Avda. Marquès de Comillas, 13.
08038 Barcelona
www.poble-espanyol.com

Ayuntamiento de
Sant Guim de la Plana
Arrabal, 1
25211 Sant Guim de la Plana
http://santguimplana.ddl.net

To the artists:

Marta Claverol
marta.claverol@gmail.com

Lourdes Perelló
pinzellades@hotmail.com

Taller del vidre
www.tallerdelvidre.com

Vitraloi
vitraloi@telefonica.net

144